Intelligent Research Design

Intelligent Research Design

A Guide for Beginning Researchers in the Social Sciences

Bob Hancké

OXFORD
UNIVERSITY PRESS

OXFORD
UNIVERSITY PRESS

Great Clarendon Street, Oxford OX2 6DP
United Kingdom

Oxford University Press is a department of the University of Oxford.
It furthers the University's objective of excellence in research, scholarship,
and education by publishing worldwide. Oxford is a registered trade mark of
Oxford University Press in the UK and in certain other countries

British Library Cataloguing in Publication Data
Data available

Library of Congress Cataloging in Publication Data
Data available

ISBN 978-0-19-957079-9

To my teachers Steve, Isabela, Stewart, Gunnar, Torben, Orfeo, Keith, Sig, Mark, Michel, Anne, and Pepper—the other students—and to my students for teaching me so much.

⬚ CONTENTS

▯ PREFACE

This short book has a long history. If it has a beginning anywhere, it started when I was involved in a pan-European doctoral training programme in political economy, called the *European Political Economy Infrastructure Consortium* (EPIC), funded by the European Commission under Framework Programme 4. The ideas developed in EPIC formed the basis for the courses on research design that I started to teach at LSE in 2000, were gradually adjusted and, I hope, improved through discussions with students from all over Europe (in London, Florence, Aix-en-Provence, and Budapest), and found their final incarnation while teaching research design and methods at the Central European University (CEU) in Budapest in the autumn of 2007. Without those courses, and especially the students who happily (I hope?) sat through them, this book would not have existed.

Many of the ideas in these pages have been in existence in some form or other as handouts that I wrote for my students', colleagues', and most of all my own benefit: rather than answering questions that appeared with diabolical frequency, I decided, I might as well write them up and distribute them. The winter break 2007–8 offered the three weeks needed to turn that disparate collection of handouts into a book draft. Between days of hiking in the hills of the Corbières, cross-country skiing in the French Pyrenees, and plenty of excellent meals (thanks Mum, Dad, Chris, Marian, David, Niki, Sarah, and Jude!), the first draft of this book slowly took shape. The comparatively light term that I enjoyed as a Visiting Professor at CEU following the winter break provided me with the time to finish and polish that draft. My sincere thanks go to the administrative and academic staff at both LSE and CEU for making professional life easy enough so that this short book could see the light.

My own teachers, especially those during my undergraduate years as a sociology student, might well chuckle if they discovered that I had written a book on research design and methods: I was neither a star in stats (or maths), and while I could hold my ground in empirical research, I never thought I would end up systematically thinking about research and teaching it. But by looking over the shoulders of my teachers when they thought about research, theirs and mine, I learnt a lot. And nothing forces you to learn as fast as teaching something—exactly what I started about ten years ago. During my own graduate student years at MIT, I slowly got acquainted with bits and pieces of what has found its way into this book, but not much was offered in a sufficiently systematic way that was easily accessible. Hence this short book—a guide on research design for beginning doctoral students. My recommendation is to read it alongside others. There are many good books on research design in university libraries these days. But very few of them address problems from the point of view of starting Ph.D. students, and some (especially King, Keohane, and Verba [1994]), are sometimes unnecessarily dogmatic in defence of their own approach and sideswipes to other views on research. And those books, like Brady and Collier (2004), which collect debates on methodology and research design in the social sciences, can be a little difficult for starting researchers.

This book tries to address these shortcomings. It is organized around the key idea that research is always *constructed* by researchers, from the moment they start until the day they finish. The social, political, and economic world is not out there, waiting to be explored by all who want to, but has to be constructed to make it amenable to research. Understanding the principles underlying this is therefore a necessary skill that has to be acquired along with substantive insights into how the world operates. Think of this book, therefore, as a friend commented, not as a cookbook, but as one that teaches you how to cook.

Despite this methodological relativism, quite a few readers might consider this to be a highly positivist guide to research. Perhaps that is the case, and if confronting strong arguments with strong empirical material counts as positivist, I do not mind pleading guilty. However, my project with this book was to filter out those points in debates over which, in my opinion, there is a reasonable consensus among researchers who are both engaged in empirical research in the social sciences. Many of my intelligent statistically inclined colleagues, for example, long for better case studies and structured comparisons because those allow them to rethink what they are doing. Most of them know and cherish the division of labour between different research traditions—they just wish, quite reasonably in my opinion, that so-called qualitative research was as methodologically self-conscious and rigorous as good statistical analysis can be. Note that I don't say much about statistical analysis in this book. There are excellent introductions that are much better than anything I could conjure up. At the start of Chapter 2, though, I present a quick glossary of very basic statistical jargon for readers with very little experience, since the chapter required it. Don't be scared: if I can write it, you can understand it. Most basic stats is, in fact, quite simple and intuitive.

The ideas in this book, as well as the examples, reflect my own professional training and preoccupations: comparative business studies and political economy, comparative politics, and European politics. Since I made an effort to keep the examples simple and straightforward, I hope they make sense to students outside these areas. But I know that colleagues who use this book may have better examples from the fields in which they are active as researchers; please send on such good examples. If I use them in a next version (hope springs eternal), I'll make sure their origin is acknowledged. I also borrow insights from several similar books that preceded it. Where the debt is substantial, I have tried to make sure it was acknowledged. But to avoid misunderstandings: without the books and articles by King, Keohane, and Verba (1994), Van Evera (1997), Hall (2004), Bates (1998), Ragin (1987), Levitt (2005) (at least as much a book on research design as on economics, by the way), Shively (2002), Brady and Collier (2004), and Dunleavy (2003), not much of this one could have been written. Where they and I disagree, they should be exonerated; where we agree, they deserve as much credit as I do. Finally, a good friend wrote and published a book on the philosophy of political economy a few months before I finished mine, in which he also addresses many of the deeper philosophical questions I raise in the first chapter. Richard Bronk's *The Romantic Economist* (Cambridge University Press 2009) disagrees in sometimes brilliant ways with me, and in ways that were not always easy to accommodate within the project I had with this book. I recommend it very warmly.

The standard advice for a book or a paper is almost invariably to write the introduction first and rewrite it at the end. For a reader of this book, this is useful advice as well: read the introduction first, and re-read it again at the end. We can then see where we disagree. If I really take seriously the idea that research is a debate, as I say in the first chapter, then this is a voice in that debate. I expect others to disagree with it; but I also expect students to learn from those disagreements, and make up their mind on their own. As long as they are thinking about their research while they are doing it, this book has served its purpose.

Thanks, without prejudice, for general discussions and on specific topics, comments on sections and on the manuscript as a whole, and for teaching me a lot by asking the right questions at the right time, go to: Nick Barr, Suzanne Berger, Richard Bronk, Steven Casper, Damian Chalmers, Steve Coulter, Tom Cusack, Michel Goyer, Max Freier, Matteo Fumagalli, Peter Hall, Dermot Hodson, Abby Innes, Erin Jenne, Alison Johnston, Jennifer Jackson-Preece, Niki Lacey, Levi Littvay, Richard Locke, Andrew Martin, Martin Rhodes, Andrew Richards, Gwen Sasse, Waltraud Schelkle, Carsten Schneider, David Soskice, Marco Simoni, Gunnar Trumbull, Christa Van Wijnbergen, Jason Wittenberg, and Stewart Wood; to two anonymous reviewers who, with different degrees of constructive criticism, helped me improve the manuscript; to Steve Coulter for help in the final stages of the manuscript; to Dominic Byatt at Oxford University Press for his encouraging support; to many friends and colleagues that I am undoubtedly and unfortunately forgetting here; and to all the students I taught over the years. One group of colleagues deserves special mention—the other residents in the WZB *Kindergarten* (Stewart Wood immortalized the expression in his own doctoral thesis), where I either learnt or realized for the first time that I learnt most of what is written up here. And, as with everything I do, Bruce and Miles were there to keep me company.

Bob Hancké
Budapest and London
December 2008

⬚ LIST OF TABLES

Introduction

Embarking on a doctorate requires, as a colleague of mine once said, a complete suspension of rationality. Think of it: you are required to write 80–100,000 words on a single topic, spread over five years or so, allow yourself, at an age when others with similar qualifications are reaching the top of the food chain, to be subjected to an examination by a group of people whose main goal that day consists of making your life difficult, and if all goes well, you are—assuming you find a job—earning between slightly and considerably less than a taxi driver in central London. Yet every year more people start doctoral studies than the previous year, and universities have started to take their Ph.D. training considerably more seriously. With few jobs and many candidates, the ability to train a young researcher well and make them write a good Ph.D. thesis has become a major pole of attraction for the best-qualified among them. And when good students go to good universities, good teachers want to be there as well.

But the devil is in the detail, as both those who teach Ph.D. students and the doctoral researchers[1] themselves find out almost immediately. Ignore the teachers: they opted for this when they signed up for a Ph.D., or at the very least when they went looking for a job in a university, and have inflicted the same pain on their own teachers—excuses from them will therefore not be accepted. For the students, things are different. Ph.D. students have a great idea—well, often they do—and think, quite reasonably, that since academia is about ideas, the thesis is pretty much written—it's just a matter of writing it up, as it were. So, they set off on their research project: they try to turn that idea into a feasible project which will allow them to make a convincing argument. But they discover quite soon that there is no reliable map to guide them, and they rightly loathe the idea of having to rely on their supervisor the whole time. This is when the Ph.D. project really starts: these doctoral researchers are about to

---

[1] I will use the words Ph.D. students, doctoral researchers, beginning researchers, etc. as substitutes in the remainder of this book.

learn the crucial skills that distinguishes doctoral (and by extension all academic) research from any other human activity on the planet. They have to start learning to think about their research while they're doing it— i.e. they have to develop some form of second-order reflexivity: reflect upon the world, and reflect upon the way they reflect upon the world.

The process by which we acquire research skills is as important as the process that allows us to develop new ideas. Let me illustrate with a few typical examples how all of this works. Very often, students start with a theory, usually a 'grand theory' that they would like to 'apply', that is, prove right by showing that it can shed light on a problem. Bourdieu's theory of how fields are structured, for example, or Weber's conception of the role of ideas in political and economic development. They then typically set out to locate an empirical area where interesting things are happening, use the concepts, explicit and implicit causalities that the theory offers, project those onto the empirical field that they have iden- tified as important, and write up what they find. Alternatively, students have a really big gripe with a prevailing orthodoxy: modernization theory in the 1960s, neoclassical economics or rational choice in political science and political economy, etc. The project then is to try to show that this way of understanding the world—often (too) loosely referred to as a theory— is 'wrong', either by demonstrating that its core assumptions do not hold, or that sometimes things happen that are incompatible with the theory. They seek to demonstrate, for example, that sometimes economic devel- opment, human development, and political development do not move in tandem, as modernization theory predicted. Or, a third way for doctoral projects to start, they start out wanting to 'prove' a statement about the world: 'EMU is a neo-liberal project', 'the welfare state is collapsing', and then spend several years amassing loads of data—sometimes truly 'all' the data they can find on this—which supposedly demonstrate that their statement about how the world really is turns out to be correct, and that by implication competing statements about the world must be wrong.

Such a project *can* lead to important insights: most alternatives to dominant theories in fact emerged and emerge in this way. Criticizing the universalistic optimism of modernization theory, for example, has led to the (re-)discovery of profound structural inequalities between different societies depending on their position in the world economy, the timing of their industrialization, and the particular form of decolonization they experienced. We also learnt that economic development, political change, and the values that people in such societies hold, can follow very different paths and evolve at very different rhythms, often undermining each other. We have learnt a lot about how modern capitalism really works by starting from the idea that economic actors do not follow the standard utility function that neoclassical economics hands them, but that their actions are embedded in institutional, cultural, or political settings that guide their behaviour. And questioning the fixed quality of preferences and identities that are at the basis of structuralist social science has led to a better understanding of how pragmatic processes with small steps can lead to novel situations. Indeed, we learnt a lot, but with a tiny number of exceptions, not from Ph.D. theses that were written in this way. Instead some elder social scientist reflected upon what he or she has learnt over his or her career, and rethought what he or she started their career with, often in an explicit or implicit conversation with a group of others who are thinking about similar problems. When we learn from Ph.D. theses, it is because they are narrow and precise, search for a causality or a functional relationship that throws into question what others have argued, and are both modest enough to see their limits and confident enough to say where a deeper point is hidden.

Why, then, are such approaches to social science problematic? Basically, they have two problems which will haunt a Ph.D. project from the start, make life very difficult for, and ultimately almost certainly beat the researcher. The first is that the link between empirical material and theory is, in these attempts, frequently underspecified. Put differently, one example that does not fit is not enough to kill a theory. When social scientists talk about empirical material, they usually refer to a set of observable implications of an argument which are gathered in a systematic way. Empirical material in this sense cannot simply be just any fact that appears to prove or disprove a theory. Instead these observable implications should ideally be collected in such a way that they are, in the limiting case, the only ones that allow the researcher to prove or disprove a theory under conditions that are set by the theory. In other words, all theories have limiting conditions, and attempts at 'proving' or 'disproving' a theory must be located within the universe of these conditions. It makes no sense, for example, to argue that rational choice perspectives cannot explain a civil war between ethnic groups in Africa. For one thing, there is a growing rational choice literature on ethnic conflicts that belies the statement. But even if you are not impressed by that literature, a reasonable claim could be made that such a case of violent ethnic strife lies on or probably beyond the outskirts of what rational choice uses as working assumptions. Such cases are likely to draw attention to deep identity divisions of a stark 'us and them' type, which makes negotiation difficult (though not necessarily impossible); possibly invokes some form of deep hatred between these groups which is hard to pin down in terms of rational calculation by actors; and war is generally considered the moment when bargaining between different groups has broken down.

The second problem with such an approach is that it will often ignore the balance between theory and empirical material in social science. In their pure form, such attempts to prove or disprove a grand theory, or make a conceptually informed statement about the world are either too theoretical, or too factual. The problems with an overly theoretical project are possibly the easiest to see: a grand theory is stated and empirical material is mobilized to illustrate that theory. But that empirical material needs a clear link to the theory in the sense alluded to above: it needs to show that it can actually be used to understand the strengths of that theory and the weaknesses of others, not that they are good examples that do not contradict the theory. The problems with an overly empirical project are the flip side of this: facts never speak for themselves, but only become meaningful because we have a new theory (argument) that makes sense of them—and, importantly, of other facts that we already knew of. If you follow this line of reasoning (which will be developed in more detail in the next chapter), research is not so much about disproving a theory but about specifying conditions under which the causalities that are implicit or explicit in the theory do not hold *at the level of generality at which the theory is defined.* We work, in other words, towards demonstrating that our argument makes the previous generation of a theory a specific instance of a wider view (Lakatos 1970). Observable implications ('data') therefore do not open a two-cornered fight between a theory and a fact, but, as Lakatos argued, a three-cornered fight between two competing arguments. (Schmitter [2008] pushes this point, suggesting that the battle is often a four-cornered one between the fact, the old theory, the new theory, and the often-ignored null hypothesis that nothing is going on.) What it implies—and this closes the circle—is that facts, even new facts which contradict an existing theory, do not settle anything in themselves. Facts are, in this universe, not even relevant unless they are organized in such a way that they systematically contradict an existing theory and simultaneously show that a new, refined version of that theory is born.

Combined, the words 'empirical' and '(social) science' therefore refer to a set of systematic relationships between the observable implications and the argument that is examined. They have to be part of the same logical universe, they should be linked in logical ways that allow us to see how a fact might undermine or strengthen a theory, and facts only make sense in light of at least two theories—the one that is rejected and the one that is upheld. This process of linking observations to theories, and thinking through which types of observations allow us to make valid statements about the implications of those theories, constitutes the core of what we call research design, and is the subject of this book.

Thinking about research design was, until quite recently, not a popular pastime in the social sciences. In large measure this was one of the effects of the growth of ever more powerful statistical techniques, which almost defined away the problem: applying more statistical controls allowed a researcher to fine-tune the fit between theory and data without worrying too much about economy of data-collection and handling. Much—possibly most—research in the social sciences, however, continued to rely on detailed narratives about individual cases or a small number of them, where the mere idea of statistical or any other controls is slightly ridiculous since—the closest thing to a crime against humanity in standard quantitative social science—the number of relevant variables usually far exceeds the number of observations.

It is, with some distance, quite remarkable that thinking about this way of making sense of social, political, and economic phenomena slowly disappeared in the post-war social sciences: relying on small numbers of cases and thinking them through in terms of their causal mechanisms and what they implied for the rest of the world was exactly what founding fathers such as Marx and Weber had done, was the basis of the method used by Robert Michels (1920) when examining political parties, and even survived into the 1950s with such classics as *Union Democracy* (Lipset et al. 1956) or *TVA and the Grass Roots* (Selznick 1949). While the tradition in the social sciences that built on small numbers of cases (the 'small-N' tradition) never entirely disappeared and certainly made significant contributions throughout this period (think of C. Wright Mills' *The Power Elite*, Graham Allison's *Essence of Decision: Explaining the Cuban Missile Crisis*, or Barrington Moore's *Social Origins of Dictatorship and Democracy*), it was not until the late 1970s that small-N research design problems made quite a dramatic appearance. Przeworski and Teune (1970), Eckstein (1975), and a handful of others raised the issues from a pure methods point of view. Theda Skocpol (1979), in turn, made explicit how this line of thinking would operate in actual research. Relying on John Stuart Mill's methods of difference and of agreement, she explored in *States and Social Revolutions* how a handful of cases could be used to disentangle complex relationships preceding revolutions and which laid the tracks for the subsequent attempts at state-building. A few years later, she put the issue more solidly on the agenda in an edited volume on method in historical sociology (Skocpol 1984). And Gary King, Robert Keohane, and Sidney Verba (1994), in their *Designing Social Inquiry*, set the broader terms of the debate on what constitutes good research design. Those second-generation trailblazing books and articles led to a wide-ranging discussion about how to use qualitative research strategies, which usually combine small numbers of cases with complex arguments, in a way that would allow them (again) to become a viable *modus operandi* in the social sciences. In *The Comparative Method*, Charles Ragin (1987) in fact started developing an alternative non-statistical analytical technique which accommodated this small-N, complex question-based universe that much qualitative social science operates in. The single most important outcome of these debates has undoubtedly been that we are all considerably more self-conscious about research design today than we have ever been.

But something else happened along the way as well. While sophisticated alternatives are discussed and published (see, e.g., Brady and Collier 2004), few of these interesting ideas on how to rethink research are translated in the practice of social research, especially among doctoral researchers, which often remains considerably less sophisticated. Some of them quickly denounce method as some form of intellectual oppression and then proceed to write an intelligent piece of commentary on the world (but not, technically, a research monograph), while others, who want to play by the rules of the game, fall back on very basic notions of research design that were *en vogue* prior to these debates, and which took the statistical model as its benchmark (King et al. 1994). A lot of the intellectual energy that is spent in excellent debates on qualitative research design just never seems to make it to the workshop of doctoral research. The second is that, despite all this attention to research design, beginning researchers still have to search hard for a book that helps them think about their own research when they start out. Most books and articles in this field disagree with others but do little in telling beginning research students how to get their own research started. Even the excellent collection in Brady and Collier (2004) requires significant prior knowledge of the debates, and rarely offers practical advice (McKeown 2004). Combined, the implicit quantitative bias in social research and the lack of accessible handbooks for beginning researchers that nudge open more research design doors, has led to a situation in which research students are told, but without so many words, that there is a (single) correct way of doing case-based 'qualitative' research.

The intellectual project of this book is to offer a slightly more eclectic approach to social research, which builds on the best insights emanating from those debates, but translated into problems that beginning researchers come across when they start out. I suggest that we treat social science as an exercise in which the different components of a project have to be permanently constructed by the researcher: the selection of a problem, the precise way a research question is stated, the presentation of the debate on that question, the gathering of empirical material to address that question, and drawing conclusions from that are the researcher's own work. A problem does not so much exist to be researched, but has to be constructed as a specific empirical research question, with strong logical links to theoretical debates. It requires an intervention from researchers to make it researchable. Think of each of the necessary elements of good research: 'the literature' does not exist before a researcher makes it his or hers and organizes the existing answers to a question into broad positions that argue with each other. Empirical material and 'cases' never present themselves as such but have to be constructed, to make sure they are valid and reliable, or as instances of a particular phenomenon by researchers. Depending on the question you ask, and the answers you want to test, cases become more or less relevant. France, for example, is not a good case to study the role of the state in capitalist economies because it is far from 'representative': the French state controlled and possibly still controls more of the economy than in most of the other G7 countries. But if you want to know what the limits of the state in a capitalist economy are, France may well be an excellent case, precisely for that reason. The limits that you discover in France are very likely to be very hard limits, possibly even near-universal, precisely because the French state controls so much of the economy. Similarly, moving from one to two cases can only be done if you remember that you are constructing a comparison, and therefore have to make explicit the dimensions along which you are comparing these two cases. And writing up what you have found is not a report of what you have done, but needs to analytically engage the initial question, literature, etc. all over again. If you think of research as ultimately being about constructing better arguments, then research design is the tool to get there.

Thinking about research in this way has two distinct advantages over the more standard positions. The first is that imposing (or better, perhaps, 'accepting') such 'subjective' moments, in which the researcher constructs the debate he or she is engaging with, the arguments he or she favours, and the link with empirical material, makes the project truly the researcher's own. Research becomes a passion fused with knowledge about theories, cases, data, and interpretations—a bit like sailing, in other words, and therefore fun. The second is what this book is about. Looking at research in this way requires learning the principles of research design in much the same way as a craft is learnt through an apprenticeship. Research requires skills and tacit knowledge in combinations that allow a researcher to think through how to approach a problem in novel ways.

The next five chapters elaborate this approach to research design in distinct steps. Before you start reading the rest of this book, be aware that all of what follows happens several times during your project: you will restate your question several times, your data and cases will require more than one iteration as well, you will keep on reading and seeing new ways to engage the literature, etc. Unfortunately, a book does not allow for such a non-linear approach: Chapter 2 follows Chapter 1, after all, as Chapter 3 follows Chapter 2 (although you don't necessarily have to read it like that). Perhaps in a later web-based version, hyperlinks might help to overcome this—although I doubt it. So, here goes for now: Chapter 1 lays the philosophical foundations of this view of research design, and translates that into how research questions are constructed. Chapter 2 translates those foundations into a series of important strategic and conceptual problems that all research faces. In Chapter 3, I discuss ways to think about very small to medium-N research designs. Chapter 4 deals with the nature of data, how to obtain them, and how to use them. Chapter 5 is about writing up the research in papers and a thesis: producing research and reproducing research are two very different things, and the chapter, I hope, helps to move from one to the other. The short final chapter sends you off on your own. The appendix gives a series of tips on the institutionalized ways in which we participate in our profession: presenting papers, discussing and reviewing papers, and writing research proposals.

1 Research in the Social Sciences

Social scientists have many goals in life. Like researchers in physics or biology they want to understand a critical problem in the world: HIV or the origins of the universe for biologists and physicists, understanding the causes of poverty or discrimination for social scientists. Social scientists are flattered if their ideas show up in policy documents, or if their arguments guide governments or international organizations in setting guidelines for intervention. But, alongside developing these substantive insights into the world, we have a slightly more down-to-earth reason for doing research: we also strive to become footnotes. For many of us, one of the biggest aims in life is to be taken sufficiently seriously by our peers so that they will cite us, either approvingly or disapprovingly. There are only so many footnotes that the world needs, though: the number of social science Ph.D. students in the world is now so large that it is simply impossible for all of them to make it to the status of a footnote in someone else's work. The process by which you become a footnote is not always fair and transparent: some small groups cite each others' work a lot and that then raises (quite artificially, in fact) their collective impact factor. But most of the time, good research helps.

What, then, is good research? Basically, there are two components to it: good ideas and good research design. It is hard to pin down how to arrive at good ideas. An insight borrowed from someone else that 'has legs', a conversation with a colleague or teacher, a paper you have read and disagree or agree with, an accidental find when you were frustrated and were looking for something else, an idea that's been brooding in some form or other, even a good novel with a glass of wine—all are possible ways to come up with good ideas. Finding good ideas may not appear easy when you start out. Very often, you may be looking at an interesting broad area but, once you sit down and try to mould it into a well-defined question, things quickly become considerably more difficult. First attempts at making these ideas explicit are often also very descriptive or very complicated. That's OK—as long as you are aware that what you have then is just that: a first attempt, which requires serious surgery along the way. On the whole, as you will discover, finding good ideas to turn into papers or a thesis becomes easier as you become more experienced. It's almost as if you begin to look at interesting events or processes through the lense of what constitutes a good question. Turning interesting observations into good ideas is one of the tacit skills you learn when you work on a Ph.D.

Good research design, the way to turn interesting ideas into excellent research, is in a formal sense easier to pin down than the process by which ideas are formed. It follows a set of rules which link question, debate, data, and argument in a convincing way—think of research design as the tool that allows you to transform a plausible point (your initial idea) into a convincing argument which gets you the Ph.D. or gets an article published. But there is a sting in the tail: once you have made your point, you are yourself a part of the literature, open to the same treatment that you gave the ones who came before you. Sadly, we not only aspire to become footnotes, we also have to live with the idea that we will be shown wrong.

How, then, do you recognize good research design? As with all judgements, you need a theory that gives you yardsticks—nothing, as they say, is as practical as a good theory. That theory is given by a crucial debate in the philosophy of science, which has the names of Karl Popper, Thomas Kuhn, and Imre Lakatos associated with it. The first section of this chapter discusses the criteria of good research that follow from that debate, that is research that contributes to scientific progress. I will then use these criteria to engage research design more directly: if we adopt a *sophisticated falsificationist* view along the lines of what Lakatos advocates, what are the practical consequences for research? The next section will start that exploration with a bird's-eye view of research design, going over its main components. The rest of this book will fill in details of that broad structure, a process that starts in the section where research questions are discussed. A short concluding section wraps up the chapter and prepares for Chapter 2.

Social science is a debate

In the broadest possible sense, the aim of the social sciences is to understand the world as it is made by human beings, the structures and institutions they produce, and the actions they take within those structures. Some of these structures and institutions have more binding sanctions associated with them than others. You may end up in jail if you commit a crime, for example, but hardly anyone will punish you severely for misspelling a word or writing an ungrammatical sentence (unless you are a lawyer, where commas can make the difference between a fortune and destitution). And the actions that people engage in may range from conforming to what the structures and institutions 'require' them to do, to subverting them by exploiting small holes in their design. Thus, the world that the social sciences tries to understand can express a high degree of regularity or be very unpredictable, depending on the tightness of the structural frameworks and the degrees of freedom that actors discover when engaging them.

For a long time, we have tried to understand this world by identifying the deep structures that made society and politics what it is. Adam Smith may well have marked one of the first universals in modern (more or less empirical) social science when he analysed and approvingly stated the inadvertent beneficial social effects of the market; in historical materialism, Marx claimed to have captured the laws of motion of history in historical materialism; and for Durkheim, the essence of industrial society was related to the new forms of division of labour that emerged in industrialism and which gave rise to anomie, a situation in which the new normative frameworks that people were subjected to were at odds with the ones they had been socialized into prior to the advent of industrial society. What connects these authors, and the many that came after them, was the notion that all of them were convinced that they were 'discovering' something about how the social world really operated, much in the same way that Newton discovered gravity, Watson and Crick (and the sidelined and almost forgotten Rosalind Franklin) DNA, and Stanley put parts of the then largely unknown continent Africa on the map. Social science, it was claimed, had finally risen out of the pre-scientific, metaphysical stage, and had become or was on the way to becoming a standard science, which inductively looked for universals: tellingly, Auguste Comte's initial term for sociology was 'social physics'.

Yet this structuralist form of logical positivism never had a complete hold on the social sciences. Max Weber was probably the first to raise the possibility that it was not the 'objective' world that influenced what we did, but that our subjective understanding of that world was at the basis of what the world looked like (and what we did in it), an approach which later was echoed in Thomas and Zaniecki's intriguing maxim (1927) that 'if men [sic] define situations as real, they are real in their consequences'; in Talcott Parsons' sociology of action; and in contemporary constructivism in its many forms. In these versions of social science, human beings were not the objects of blind historical forces, but subjects that shaped institutions, structures, and therefore the social and political world as we know it. In this tradition, social science is less about uncovering the deep structure of society and politics, and much more—almost exclusively, in fact—about understanding how the world was 'made' through the meaning that actors gave to the different elements of the social world. Understanding the world as a social scientist required, in this view, putting yourself in the position of the actor, seeing the world as he or she did, and thus making sense of their actions.

Since its early days, social science has had within it competing visions of both how the social and political world is constituted—what, in other words, its driving forces and their effects are (its ontology)—and how we can develop empirical knowledge about that world (its methodology) (Hall 2004). When doing their work, social scientists always implicitly or explicitly started from what some of their predecessors had said. Weber's famous essay on the *Protestant Ethic and the Spirit of Capitalism* could be and has been read as a direct engagement of the Marxist theory of capitalism as the result of a class struggle. Marx's theory, in turn, was developed in an argument with Hegel's dialectical idealism and Smith's invisible hand. And Durkheim's *Suicide* starts with a review of more or less plausible alternative explanations of trends and levels in suicide that others came up with before him. It is a fair bet that you can read any serious classic book in the social sciences and discover that its author, whatever the tradition they were working in, profoundly disagreed with some point made by others and then went on to prove their own point. And, when reading a published article today, it takes not more than a few minutes to discover that the piece is written as much against someone else as it is in favour of the author's point. Even the most hard-core statistical paper is incomplete without an explicit acknowledgment of the points with which the author agreed or disagreed *before* the analysis started.

The basic architecture of the social sciences is therefore that of a *debate*, in which authors try to show each other wrong by coming up with better logical constructions of arguments, more accurate data, or a combination of the two. A better specification of the conditions under which a theory applies is an example of a better argument, since it shows that the previous theory was a special instance of the more general one that you implicitly advocate. Whilst most sciences today have the structure of a debate, this definition of the field as a debate has, because of the multi-paradigmatic character of the social sciences, been a perennial, eye-catching characteristic of the social sciences. Despite what we often learn in our undergraduate years, social science is, therefore, not about finding a hidden structure to society or discovering deep trends that no one else has seen, but about disagreeing with someone by building arguments that show them wrong.

Science in general, and social science in particular, is a special type of debate, however. It is not just about disagreeing with an existing argument or theory, but about *solving puzzles*. Take Weber's essay as an example. He studied the emergence of capitalism in America, which was one of the first fully developed capitalist nations, both for Marxists and in light of the prevailing wisdom at the time, and *then* demonstrated there was a strong affinity between belief systems and the development path of the economy. Precisely because the United States could convincingly be construed as the pinnacle of capitalist development in the nineteenth century, demonstrating that even in this 'most advanced' case of capitalism normative conceptions rather than class struggles seemed to drive economic development, posed a profound puzzle for the standard Marxist view (cf. also Hamilton [1996]). Puzzles are, in other words, questions of a special nature: they have the potential to shake the foundations of the answers that have been given before, because they raise a question that should have been answered by existing theories but was not. In principle, they can take many shapes, from a single fact that is aberrant in light of the predictions of that particular theory, to a paradox, as when in two cases (A and B) the opposite happened from what the theories suggested would happen (X in A and Y in B), and the outcomes appear, as it were, misaligned given what we knew about the world (outcome Y should have belonged to A, not to B, and the other way around). Whatever exact shape they take, puzzles always relate directly to the theory or argument that is under fire, and are located within the universe as the theory proposes it.

In a few small steps we have learnt a lot about what constitutes research in the social sciences. It is about *engaging a debate* (not about finding a hidden law of society), through the *construction of puzzles* that engage a theory on its own terrain (and not just by disagreeing and coming up with an alternative answer), and about finding the *most convincing solution* to the puzzle (relying on a combination of logic and data). This view of social science as resolving puzzles has important consequences for how to approach research. Many beginning social scientists want to show an established theory 'right' and go in search of facts that prove the theory right. Assume for a moment that they succeed in this: what have they contributed to our understanding of the world? In the old positivist model, they have contributed quite a lot: they have shown, after all, that a theory—a set of understandings of the world which are causally connected—explained the facts that they presented the theory with. For a 'puzzler', however, nothing has changed: the researcher has simply contributed a data point to an existing established theory which confirms that theory. Now, as the puzzlers then wryly point out, since we already knew that the theory was able to handle such facts, we do not know anything now that we did not know before. By its very nature, social science as 'puzzling' implies that we try and show up an existing argument or theory, not that we all contribute to it (cf. Crouch [2005: 5]).

This point is known as the '*verificationism* versus *falsificationism*' debate. Since it is quite counterintuitive when you first encounter it, let's take it step by step. Popper (1959, 1989) started the debate by raising concerns over the fact that theories can often explain many instances of a phenomenon. Such theories emphasize the congruence between facts and theory, ironically even when the facts contradict each other. Psychoanalysis can explain, for example, why a father would want to drown his child *and* why he would jump into the water to save it, just as Marxism can explain both rebellion *and* acquiescence by workers. Since their explanatory power is high, that seems to make them strong theories. However, a theory that can explain all possible recurrences of a phenomenon, Popper pointed out, lacks one crucial component: it will never encounter facts that would demarcate that theory from another one. Confirming an established theory therefore tells us little about how strong that theory really is. For confirmation to work, it has to be 'risky' in Popper's words (1989: 33–7): it should make explicit which facts are incompatible with the theory or hypothesis. 'Irrefutability of a theory [the ability of a theory to predict every possible event—BH] is not a virtue of a theory (as people often think), but a vice' (Popper 1989: 36). Testing a theory therefore requires that the theory or hypothesis are posited in falsifiable terms; only under these circumstances can confirmation be taken as preliminary support for that argument.

The consequence is that confirming an existing established theory (not a contested one, note, which is part of a debate) is a zero marginal contribution to the development and progress of science, because we already knew, implicitly or explicitly, what we now claim to have discovered. Verificationism, the process by which we *verify* (as in 'show the truth of') a theory, cannot be scientific progress if we define the latter as developing new knowledge about the world. If, say, the prevailing theory is that economic development leads to democratic consolidation, then finding a case in which economic development leads to democratic consolidation is, in these terms, exactly the same as not having done anything at all. Science, remember, does not operate on the model of elections, where a majority carries the argument—where, *mutatis mutandis*, an additional data point strengthens a theory—but works on logical grounds. The model of the rational utility-maximizer at the basis of economics and rational choice theory, to take an example, is there because of its logical power and its heuristic function, not—or not just—because many political scientists and economists have adopted it as their basic model. The only way you can 'push the boundaries of science', supposedly what a Ph. D. is all about, is by coming up with a set of facts that no one else has come up with, and thus *falsifying* (as in 'demonstrating the falseness of') an existing theory. Take the example above: if you came up with a country that had been poor for a while yet had a democratic political system, or a country that was rich and not democratic, you have produced a puzzle for the standard theory, which we can then re-examine.

But, as Kuhn (1962) pointed out, theories often do not behave that way. Scientific theories retain their appeal to those who work within them even a long time after they have been proven wrong to everyone else. Kuhn rationalized this observation by saying that such theories go through a two-step process: for a long time, researchers are contributing to an existing theory, even when that theory begins to deviate from facts that researchers collect. In fact, the way researchers look at the world filters data to such an extent that ill-fitting or contradictory observations are discarded as inconsequential anomalies, and where they cannot be ignored, they are incorporated with the help of ancillary hypotheses. Eventually, though, important facts no longer fit the theory, and a new theory is developed that can encompass both the old and the new facts, and the old theory is discarded: a paradigmatic revolution has taken place. The main reason why researchers do not drop the old theory at the first sighting of a new, problematic fact is simply that they stick together, in the *belief* that one aberrant fact can safely be ignored.

Take the set of hypotheses, popular in both academic and policy-making circles, that says that more flexible labour markets will lead to lower unemployment. The idea is based on a simple model of the labour market, in which a flexible wage will go up or down in response to demand for labour: if the economy slows down and firms produce less, wages fall to the point where it makes sense for companies to hire workers (or not lay them off), and everyone who wants a job has one, at the prevailing wage; if the economy grows, firms need more labour, and wages rise as a result, to the point where all those who want to work, can do so. Institutions in a political economy such as collective bargaining or generous welfare systems play an important role here, since they stop wages from adjusting flexibly. The effect, according to these theories, is higher unemployment than a labour market that clears would produce. In some form or other, this model has been a cornerstone of many analyses of unemployment in the last two decades (see, for the more sophisticated versions, Layard et al. [1991]; Nickell and Van Ours [2000]). Yet, if you take a careful look at the data, it turns out that the claim has very little empirical support (Baker et al. 2004). The statistics are often very weak, at best tentative rather than conclusive, and most economists are hard-pushed to come up with a single example to show that, when controlling for every other possible explanation such as macroeconomic policy, real and nominal exchange rate depreciations, and more generally economic growth, the relation between deregulated labour markets and unemployment holds. Notwithstanding its generally weak basis, as even some of the OECD economists admit today (Bassanini and Duval 2006), the argument is not about to be abandoned. Doing so would imply letting go of one of the basic tenets of standard (neoclassical) economics that says that ultimately markets clear.

At a higher level of abstraction, that of Kuhn's paradigms, a similar process takes place. Marxism, for example, has been falsified in more than one crucial way: none of the places where socialist revolutions occurred were among the most advanced capitalist nations (the main socialist revolutions in human history, in the USSR and China, in fact, simply skipped capitalism altogether at the time of the revolution and are now discovering a rather unpleasant version of it), and many socialist economies have produced inefficiencies that are incompatible with the ideas of human progress underlying socialism (but note that some key Marxist insights into the structure of capitalist society, such as class analysis, may well remain a highly useful tool for understanding the world today). Despite the theory being falsified in two of its key predictions, Marxism still exists, often justified by the idea that capitalism produces ever more contradictions, which lead to crises (not really a contentious claim in 2008 and 2009), and that therefore the theory has not yet been proven wrong in its basic tenets. In other words, Marxism as a theory of the world is alive and well among social scientists despite its demonstrable failures to explain the last two centuries of capitalist development. The irony is that this hits Popperian falsificationism in its key predictions: according to the falsificationist argument, Marxism is a prime candidate for theoretical extinction, yet it refuses to go under.

These examples bring us to what is now considered as the cornerstone of the modern philosophy of social science, and will allow us to complete the circle that we started at the beginning of this section. The theory that helped us a long way to resolving this problem is associated with the name of Imre Lakatos. The argument that Lakatos (1970) developed is that both Popper and Kuhn got something important right: Popper was correct in his reliance on falsification as the key to scientific progress, and Kuhn was right in his observation that scientists cling to defunct theories even in the light of falsification. But Lakatos also pointed out that Popper was rather naïve in his view of falsificationism, since theories never totally collapse on the basis of one aberrant fact, while Kuhn to some extent merged a sociology of science and a philosophy of science. Theories have two very different components, according to Lakatos. The one we all know well, and which is at the basis of all empirical science, is the part that produces (testable) predictions: Lakatos called them *'theories'*—we could also call them hypotheses. These are different from the second component which we do not necessarily know, in large part because it is hidden from view: the core of the *'research programme'*, which, in turn, produces these theories and hypotheses. Research programmes operate in the background, and from it theories (or hypotheses) emanate which can be verified or falsified. When a theory T1 is falsified, it does not just end up in the dustbin of history, as Popper claimed, but lives on as a reformulation T2 with different predictions, taking into account what has been falsified. Since in the debates that we have in the social sciences we never actually touch the research programme but only the theories that it produces, what we call a theory never entirely disappears but finds reincarnations in a new set of falsifiable predictions.

To take the earlier example: the view that flexible labour markets lead to lower unemployment is recast by its proponents by adding hypotheses that qualify the view but do not reject it: under conditions of fast growth, for example, or of very expansive fiscal policy, unemployment can be low even if labour markets are not very flexible, because the positive effect of one offsets the negative effect of the other. And Marxism is alive and well, in this view, not because Marxists 'believe' in it more than standard economists 'believe' in the utility-maximizing individual, but because at the level at which we engage it, it has been reformulated to accommodate new facts, and has the potential to keep on doing so for a long time. And all the while, the research programme of Marxism, which lays down the basic causalities of the theory at the highest possible level of abstraction, remains untouched. This insight helps us understand not only why theories survive against the odds, but also why debates are never fully settled—or, put differently, why social science will always be constructed around debates. If a theory appears falsified, it is likely to pop up behind you, like Mr Smith (the bad guy in *The Matrix*), start another assault from a slightly different position, and the debate starts all over again.

The upshot of this view of science is that facts in themselves never really settle debates, as Popper suggested. For a theory (as in 'T1' and 'T2' above, not as in 'research programme') to be proven wrong, we need more than facts: we need a new theory. In the now well known words of Lakatos, (social) science is not engaged in two-cornered fights between a theory T1 and an aberrant fact F, but in three-cornered fights between T1, F, and T2. Scientific progress does not consist in showing a theory T1 wrong, but in showing that T2 not only accommodates all the facts already known under T1, but also the new and aberrant fact F. A new theory has to be, in other words, at least as good as the old one, *and* know how to handle a new fact that sits within the universe as T1 understands it. But that also means that our knowledge of the world is always provisional: the explanation we give for a particular phenomenon is the best we (think we) can come up with for now, not the last word.

Two immediate practical implications for beginning researchers follow from this discussion. The first is that since we can never directly engage the research programme underlying a theory, our arguments have to be formulated in such a way and at an appropriate level of abstraction where they can be proven wrong: when compared with observations drawn from reliable data, the proposition can in principle be shown to be false. Conversely, since we cannot disprove a research programme (or a grand theory, a slightly different word for research programme) because we never deal with it directly, we should engage its (falsifiable) manifest-ations in empirical social science. For example, it is somewhat irrelevant whether you think neoclassical economics is wrong or not; you simply cannot directly attack that theoretical construct. But you can demonstrate that some of its predictions, for example, that OECD economies need to liberalize their labour markets in order to bring unemployment down, are wrong.

The second implication is that we should concentrate on the search for causal mechanisms rather than of deep trends in society (Elster 1989). 'Deep trend' statements are those that claim that a universal phenomenon is playing itself out, often monotonically rising or falling, usually without a clear specification of why this is the case. Good examples of such a trend are 'globalization'—increased global trade, the worldwide integration of finance, and the emergence of a global culture in the shape of cities and fashion—or the global trend towards liberal democracy that quite a few optimistic political scientists thought to have identified in the 1990s. The discussion on the nature of social science as a debate already hinted at the problematic aspects of such a way of understanding the world; armed with Popper's and Lakatos' insights we can now state this point more formally: a statement of a deep trend is, in a way, either too easily falsifiable—with one aberrant fact—or entirely unfalsifiable, in the sense that you can always find instances that support it. In a way, when you say that something deep seems to be going on, you ask the reader and listener to suspend his or her critical faculties and accept that you have seen something that no one else has seen. This may be the case, but observed parts of a 'trend' have the deeply annoying characteristic that they tell you little about the future. An upward sloping curve over time, until today, can keep on rising in the future (the 'trend' that you advocate), stabilize at the level where it is and flatten out, or even fall after a while (both of which would contradict your argument). Unless you have a good explanation for why the trend line will do what you predict, your assertion—this is not really an 'argument'—has a very weak basis. But such an explanation can only take the form of a causal mechanism; you would do much better to cut out the middleman and go straight to the causality you are interested in.

With these last two points, we have moved squarely into the area at the core of this book. How do we translate these principles of 'puzzling' and 'falsifying' into research design for empirical social science? The remainder of this chapter will slowly leave this elevated discussion behind, and adapt a more practical approach. I start with a general overview of research design, and then discuss how to think about your research question. While the text moves away from the rather abstract points made until now, the principles underlying philosophy of science will stay with us all along and regularly show up in the remainder of this book when we encounter a particularly pernicious problem—so do not erase it from your RAM yet.

From puzzling and falsifying to research design

Research design is a crucial ingredient of science. If you evaluate a drug, you need clinical trials, possibly experiments, and definitely some form of inferential statistics to assess its effects. If you think smoking is bad for you, you need to assemble a random sample of smokers and non-smokers and see whose health is better, if possible controlling for all other factors that may produce bad health. If your goal is to find out how women are treated in the workplace, you compare women and men (yes, women and men—think about why) in several professions on a relevant scale and check for the effects of sex, occupation, and possible interactions between the two (it is possible, for instance, that women are treated considerably worse at the bottom of the occupational scale than at the top: think of cleaners versus corporate lawyers). In all these instances, you try and link systematic observations about questions to causal arguments—that is the core of research design. Research design offers you a structure that guides you in organizing what you want to know about the world so that you can delineate what you are doing, intervene in a debate, and position yourself in it.

Think of research design as a craftsman's toolbox, not a rigid set of prescriptive rules: what you do with it, is ultimately up to you—you ask your question, and organize the debate around it; the link between your question, your answer, and your data and cases, are all in your hands. Research therefore has a large inherently subjective component. But that does not mean that anything goes: there are principles of research design. These principles, which are detailed in what follows in this section and this book, ought to help you in distinguishing between strong and weak research questions, structuring and presenting debates, making logical arguments, selecting data and/or cases, and building and using comparisons to make better arguments.

Research starts with a question. Research does not start with a literature review, or with data in search of a question, but ultimately with a question that sheds new light on answers that others have given before. The research process is answering that question. A good way of getting this right is to think about research that you are doing not as a topic or a theme, but as a question—when someone asks you what you are doing, avoid answering that question by saying 'I work on...', but by saying 'I am asking the question why...' or 'I am trying to understand how...'.

Your research question has to fulfil some criteria. The next section goes into considerably more detail on how research questions are constituted, but the basics can be stated here. Probably the most important one is that it needs to be asked in such a way that you can be wrong. There must be a chance that reliable data you will find tell you that the answer that you were thinking of giving to the question you are asking is not the right answer. Simplicity (derived from 'simple', not 'simplistic'!) is a second characteristic of research questions. You can think of this in two ways. One is the 'grandmother test': you ought to be able to explain to your grandmother what you are doing, why it matters, and what you think is going on (what the possible answers are). Another way to think about this is to imagine that you are at a party with graduate students from other departments. Imagine explaining to them what you are trying to find out, but without using the sometimes hermetic jargon that prevails in your discipline.

A question implies answers. You are never the first to think about a problem. Since the last two millennia of intellectual history were not just wasted time for humanity until you came along, write a literature review that reflects that. If you are scared of taking on the last 2,000 years, then start at least with the past decade or so. At its most basic level, your literature review should allow you to identify the main broad positions on your question (usually not more than two to four) and the debate that followed it—and you should do that in a subtle and intellectually honest way, that is, without building a straw man that can be blown over with just one gasp of air. The literature review, in other words, is your construction of the competing answers to your question, that is, the theories that you consider yourself up against.

This summary statement suggests what a literature review should not be, but, alas, too often is: a borderless and aimless wander through books and articles, primarily to show some imaginary reader (usually your supervisor) that you really know the field and have done your homework. However, your supervisor works on the assumption that you more or less know the area, and will help you where he or she thinks things could improve, so trying to impress him or her is unnecessary. Remember also that others who will read this (as some of your supervisor's colleagues have to do if your department has some form of collective evaluation of doctoral research) are usually not very impressed by the extent of your knowledge of the literature. They all assume that you know what you know. In fact, they can quite justifiably claim that you should not be where you are if you did not master this literature. Secondly, you are bound to read a lot more than you need for your research. That is too bad in the short run, but be aware that this makes you a better researcher and teacher in the long run, since you have a large reservoir of relevant literature at your fingertips. In the immediate, however, the returns on all that work may be meagre; live with that redundancy, dump what you do not need for this project, and jot down interesting ideas in a separate file for future consumption. Keep literature reviews focused, analytical, and above all as short as possible.

Engage the debate. Research, as we saw, consists of engaging a debate. It builds on existing research by contradicting it. If the function of the literature review was to construct that debate, and show where the weaknesses lie in the sense that existing positions are unable to come to terms with the (aberrant) data you present, this is the point where you take the reins. You have to delineate your position from that of the others in the debate, but without exaggerating. Again, think of the last 20–2,000 years of science as something to learn from. You will notice that the more clearly your initial research question was specified, the easier it is to mark the differences between you and the others, and to see what they have contributed to what you are thinking.

Contributions to such debates follow a few principles. The first is the principle of parsimony: start by saying as much as possible with as few explanatory tools as possible and complicate things afterwards. It makes no sense to draw up a list of all the causes that you can identify to explain something. A list is not an argument, but a handy tool for shopping—treat it like that. An argument that explains more variation than the one you are up against is a stronger argument. Marxist explanations of imprisonment, for example, often allude to some form of control of the reserve army of labour (the part of the active population that is not in jobs now, but can easily be mobilized if unemployment rates fall too much and workers gain too much power as a result). However, since this is supposedly a general characteristic of capitalist economies, the argument has a very hard time accounting for different levels of prison populations across OECD economies, especially those with similar levels of unemployment. Any political–economic explanation of different levels of imprisonment must therefore go beyond the idea that they are a tool for controlling the working class (thanks go to Nicola Lacey for this example). Conversely, an argument that explains less is a weaker argument, even if it seems to be more 'realistic'. If your argument truly captures reality better than others, then that should be expressed as a puzzle, an aberrant fact that does not fit with the prevailing theories. Science, including social science, is a way of reducing complexity, not a descriptive device.

Secondly, carefully think through if your argument on the specific case that you are studying also tells you something about other cases. If it does, all the better; if it does not, check if (at the very least) it helps understand or explain the best case for the argument that you are up against. If it does not, dump the argument: something which tells us less than what we know already is not a contribution to a debate. Normally, this is the point where your colleagues and supervisor(s) give you the best advice you can get: don't do it. Frustrating, yes, but also necessary: research design improves if you think of your research as organizing the cards in such a way that they are stacked against you and you still come out on top.

Finally, if your argument is complex and has many different dimensions, it becomes (on the principle of simplicity mentioned earlier) hard to read, digest, and understand. Such arguments often show up as lists—and, unless you actually go shopping, avoid those. What you need to do then is search for a reorganization of the argument by identifying an organizing principle that sorts out the different parts of what you are saying. That overarching principle then becomes the core point, and the 'list' is a collection of specific expressions of that point.

From debate to empirics. Once you have established what your question is, what the answers are that you are trying to come to terms with—both yours and theirs—and have thought through how yours differs from what has been said up until now, the biggest and arguably the most difficult step in research design follows. You have to think of how to build these alternative views on the question into the empirical research you will be doing: from now on, your research starts to move between an explicit and an implicit engagement of those other positions. The way to do that is to search for data and cases which simultaneously address your hypothesis *and* the others in the debate. Here's why: when you have reached the stage where you are thinking about what others have said and what you think is wrong with that, it probably is relatively easy to find good examples that prove your point; it might be equally easy to find cases which disprove others. But that will not do: 'for example' is not an argument. Ideally, you should be looking for data of some sort which simultaneously lead to a refutation of the others, and to a convincing or at least plausible proof of your point. A simple example: imagine you disagree with the idea that economic development produces democracy. A country that is poor and that has not grown much in the last few decades (examine both *levels* of economic development and *rates* of change), but which has features that we associate with a democracy (e.g. equal participation of citizens, open debate, and some form of organized opposition) might be a good case for you to explore. Imagine that you discover that the political system involves ancient traditions of decision-making that include all citizens directly or indirectly. That case suggests that sometimes democracy can emanate from long-standing traditions regardless of the level of economic development. This is a good case to study, because it not only questions the standard theory that you are up against on its own terms (poor countries can be democracies) but also offers an alternative path to democracy. Exploring the way this country operates is almost certain to shed a new light on the link between economic development and democracy.

When you reach such a point in your research, pause for a moment to savour it. You are now beginning to think like a researcher, since implicitly you are asking a crucial question: 'if I am right and the others are wrong, what would I have to find, and if I am wrong and the others are right, what would I have to find?' This way of thinking, in terms of *observable implications*, distinguishes the initial idea that you had from the research project that you are engaged in now. Both may still look and feel the same to you, but you have made a gigantic leap, since you are now confronting your and other ideas with systematic data of some sort. Observable implications are therefore rightly considered the cornerstone of good empirical research design (and the words should be framed above your desk). Our ideas are usually quite abstract, parsimonious, and couched in conceptual terms. But such abstract parsimonious concepts are not running down the street, ready to be recognized by every passer-by. These concepts and the causalities they imply therefore need to be operationalized in a way that allows you to think through how your argument relates to and is different from other arguments in the debate. This leads to the central insight I alluded to earlier: if a causal mechanism that you champion leads to exactly the same predicted observable implication as one that you are up against, your argument is, in Lakatosian terms, not a new theory, since there is nothing that you predict that another theory has not predicted. This problem of *observational equivalence* is possibly the most important practical outcome of the Lakatos–Kuhn–Popper debate that I discussed earlier in this chapter. Sophisticated falsificationism implies that you have to find a set of systematically collected data (in the broadest sense of the word) that contradict an existing theory; if data are commensurate with two theories, you have not found that (yet) and you have to go back to the drawing board.

There you are, then: question, debate, argument, and cases are organically linked into one seamless research design. Your question, your literature review, your argument, and your data and case selection all follow logically from each other and speak to each other. They are like a diamond which you can enter at any point and see the whole thing in slightly different terms (see Schmitter [2008]). At this point, do not worry too much if there are still loose ends. You now know pretty well where you are going, even if you did not get all the details right. It is almost certain that your question will go through a few changes over the next few years, and quite likely that you realize that the empirical material you relied on is not as good as it looked. And along the way you will discover new arguments that you underestimated or ignored at the start. So be it. You will correct that as you hone your research, and when you start writing up (see Chapter 5), you have a chance to make this all work again, but with carefully chosen words. Remember that you are engaged in a highly creative exercise, and you have to allow yourself some freedom to make mistakes so that you can improve things.

What is a research question?

Constructing a research question is the first and arguably the most important part of your research. With some overstatement, you could say that getting the question right is half the work of a thesis. It guides your literature review, it suggests the type of answers you can give, informs you where to find data that will allow you to prove others wrong while you make your point, and is a strong disciplining device when you think about how to write up your research. Over the years, I developed a set of criteria which apply to practically all research questions that address an empirical project. Most of these follow from my experience, both as a graduate student and as a teacher, but they can quite easily be linked back to the discussions that preceded this section. Remember, though, that you never get your question right the first time around. As you delve into empirical material, new dimensions show up that make you rethink what you were doing, and you change your question slightly. Developing a research question is an iterative process—learn to live with that. The other thing to keep in mind when you start off is not to put all your thesis eggs in one basket. Once you have hit upon something that looks like a feasible project, try several slightly different questions and approaches to the problem that you are interested in. See how the question might work out if you relied on case studies, on statistical analysis, on structured comparisons, etc. Each of these approaches has its own strengths and weaknesses, and may lead to slightly different research questions.

Relevance. A research question has to be relevant to real-world problems. Write up in a few words why it matters to ask and answer this question in the first place. Think of this as the 'so what?' question. What are the policy dimensions, political considerations, and academic literature that you will engage? Beware of gaps in the literature. They are usually there for a very good reason, and they do not necessarily offer a strong basis for good research questions.

Pre-research. No research question can be constructed in an armchair. Even if you are brilliant, it is impossible to claim that democratization is contingent upon economic development without at the very least having gone to the library and found some data that allowed you to check some easy and hard cases for the argument (i.e. see if poor countries are more likely to be undemocratic and the other way around, and think through what else may cause this correlation). All good research questions are the product of a prior engagement with empirical material. That explains why beginning doctoral students seem to have a hard time finding a good question and their teachers usually much less so: as we accumulate knowledge, we discover an increasing number of aberrant facts that could be used as the basis for a research question. It also explains why the final version of the research question usually emerges at the end of your project: at that point you actually know what you have found and are able to recast the initial question accordingly.

Three-cornered fight. A research question has to engage an existing debate in such a way that it shows that a crucial dimension of the problem was ignored by previous generations of researchers. Solid research questions usually take the form of puzzles. A puzzle is, as we saw, a set of systematic observations that are at odds with the prevailing understanding of the world. Puzzles meet all the *a priori* criteria that Lakatos imposed on scientific progress: they involve a clear statement of the theory prior to the research, an unexpected observation that cannot be accommodated within that theory, and they invite an answer that both differs from the prevailing ones and builds on them by showing that the answer to the puzzle makes the previous generation of answers wrong in some way.

Beginning researchers often mistake more or less interesting questions for a puzzle. For example, they discover that after the split of Czechoslovakia in 1993, the Czech Republic rapidly opened up to foreign capital while the Slovak Republic did so much more slowly, ask why this happened, and then state that in their research proposal as a puzzle they have discovered. There is no doubt that this is an interesting observation—but it is not (yet) a puzzle unless the question and the debate can be reconstructed in such a way that we would expect both the Czech Republic and Slovakia to be doing the same thing with regard to foreign investors. To turn this question into a puzzle therefore requires presenting the two cases so that, on the basis of some prior understanding of the world, usually those following from a literature review, we would expect them both to follow a similar trajectory. Puzzles do not, therefore, so much exist but have to be constructed rhetorically.

Concreteness and abstraction. Try and formulate questions which are as close to the empirical material as possible without being merely descriptive: your question should ideally be a specific, empirically informed instance of a more general question in the broad area that you study. When you have a few versions of the question you are asking, sit back and take a hard look at them, using the following yardsticks: Is the question concrete enough? Does it address an empirical puzzle or issue? Can you move up the ladder of abstraction and show that the empirical question is a special instance of a broader issue? Questions for which you answer these queries with 'no' should be reformulated or evacuated. The degree of focus of the question is a parallel problem. Can you distinguish between this question and another one that you might want to ask? If not, you'll find that you cannot answer it without dragging in all kinds of other things.

Falsifiability. A research question needs to be asked in such a way that you can be wrong (and that you know when you are wrong): when confronted with systematic reliable data, the answer to the question should be such that it can, in principle, be shown to be wrong. Make sure, therefore, that a research question is not a statement, and that it should allow different possible answers. 'Populism is rampant in Central Europe' is a statement, not a question, and hard to disprove. There is certainly a lot of populist politics going on in Central Europe, but it is not clear what you would have to find to conclude that populism is not 'rampant'—is the populist glass half full or half empty? Better to ask a more precise question: 'Are mainstream parties in Central Europe [or in one of the CEE countries] adopting populist platforms?' Such narrower, more precise questions often also allow you to think through what the elements in your argument would be: 'Yes, mainstream parties in Central Europe are adopting populist platforms, because [*and here follows your argument*]' or 'No, they don't, because [*your argument or counterargument*]'.

Simplicity. A question needs to be simple (not simplistic). Try the grandmother or party test mentioned earlier: can you explain to colleagues in other departments or to your grandmother what you are trying to do? Far too many of us think that we need complicated ideas expressed in complicated words. Beside the obvious counterpoint that long complicated words simply look and sound bad and take up more space, they are often unnecessary and even counterproductive, since they may hide quite trivial points or, worse, confused thoughts under a barrage of words. Compare the following two versions of a question: (*a*) 'Does socio-economic development require the prior democratic consolidation of the extant political arrangements?'; (*b*) 'Does democracy make nations wealthier?' Both address the same basic mechanism: the median voter in a wealthy market economy may have an income below the mean ('average'; see Table 2.1 for definitions of statistical measures), democracy usually leads to more redistribution, and this, in turn, leads to higher spending by lower-income groups, which results in higher demand and therefore higher growth. But the second version of the question is a lot easier to understand than the first, even though the first sounds more like 'academese'.

Researchability. A question has to be researchable. The three dimensions below are far from exhaustive, but they do offer useful pointers. First of all, are there data you can use to answer your question and do you have access to them? Imagine that you deductively know exactly what the case(s) you need should look like. But when you start looking around for them, you discover that the case does not exist. Or worse: the material exists, but the CIA is sitting on what you need for your thesis; assess the chances that the CIA is going to comply with your request for sharing data before you start. Secondly, are the data in principle available to others? Imagine that you can obtain good material from a secret conversation behind closed doors; that type of evidence is not admissible in the social sciences, since no one else can have access to those data. In our trade, we do not take things on trust, and few of us are after a scoop the way journalists are. We require data to be verifiable, so see how you can assure or increase verifiability, even if you have privileged access to sources. Ideally, sources should be open to all who want to explore them. For a variety of reasons that may not always be possible; on those occasions, you should be extremely transparent at the very least, and rely on your judgement (and that of colleagues and supervisors) to decide how to use the source. Thirdly, is your question limited in time or space? Does it have a clear geographic area, a starting point in time, and a clear and logical 'end' that you work towards and explain/answer? Or are you chasing a moving target? Imagine that you are fascinated by developments in the Middle East today (2009) and plan to do research on it. The best advice you can get is not to do it: the region you are interested in is likely to look very different in the near future, and even if it is not (in your opinion), you cannot be sure. When I started graduate studies in the late 1980s, quite a few of my friends and colleagues were fascinated with Germany. A small incident in Berlin in November 1989 meant that many of them found themselves suddenly studying a different country. Asking what led to the fall of the Berlin Wall in 1989 is a researchable question which can lead to a feasible project; studying the effects of the events of 1989 was probably much less so in the 1990s, and possibly still in the 2000s.

Positive outcomes. Ask questions about things that have actually happened, not about things that have not happened (yet). The future cannot be studied (unless you have gifts no one else possesses, but then you might want to ask yourself what you are doing at a university). Several years ago, before the EU enlargement of May 2004, one of my students came up with the question what would happen to the organization of Poland's border controls when it joined Schengen. My reaction was that, even though Poland was admittedly likely to join Schengen in the foreseeable future, there were too many blank spots and unpredictable events in the world as we knew it then to answer this question, and I advised the student to drop it. In a similar way, finding out why France does not do more to reform its labour markets can be interesting, but since you are asking why something did *not* happen, the answer is almost certainly *overdetermined*: the role of the state in the economy; the nature of the political system; the strength (or, perhaps better, hidden weakness) of trade unions; the popular abhorrence of neo-liberally coloured solutions; and the lack of viable forums where state, employers, and trade unions can negotiate reforms are all possible answers to the question, and *ex ante* all are equally plausible. So, rephrase your question by finding a comparable country on these dimensions, and where reforms happened, and then filter out the factors both countries share by asking why the other country reformed its labour markets when France did not. The comparator functions as a limiting principle in this case, and it allows you to specify your question on France in a way that helps understand which ingredient(s) of the French socio-political system are responsible for blocking reform in the labour market.

Studying why something did not happen should only be done if the counterfactual world is, in theory, extremely well known. For example, since Florence was one of the centres of Renaissance capitalism, and since early centres often have advantages that would keep them in that central place, why did Florence not become the point of gravity of eighteenth- and nineteenth-century capitalism (Emigh 1997)? The implicit counterfactual that is handed to you by these insights may be useful in understanding what went wrong in Florence in, say, the sixteenth century that precluded it from becoming the centre of the modern capitalist world.

Parsimony. Try answering the question you are asking; ideally you should be able to do so without relying on lists of factors that 'clearly' matter. Questions that produce answers which appear as lists, are usually not good questions. By all means avoid invoking some combination of ideas, interests, and institutions as part of your answer. There is an unimaginably small chance that you are wrong unless God's hand was involved: you have just claimed that what you are interested in is explained by practically everything that matters in the social world (ideas, interests, and institutions).

But parsimony does not mean being simplistic. There are, as we now know, many ways to become a capitalist democracy: through mass suffrage and organized labour movements; as a result of a national revolution in a decentralized economy; having it imposed by outside occupying powers or international organizations, etc. Reflecting that variety in your research is likely to lead to answers that combine many factors and processes. Excessive parsimony would lead you to discard many that vary across cases, and you could discover that all cases you look at share one factor. Be sensitive to the fact that this single factor may require the presence of some of those you discarded to play the role you attribute to it. Economic development, for example, is, as far as we can tell, not a necessary condition for democracy. But there is little doubt that, once a country is a democracy, economic growth sustains that arrangement. An ultra-parsimonious approach to this question would probably miss that dynamic effect, since it would discard the very high correlation between economic development and (remaining) democratic.

Conclusion

This chapter laid the foundations for the rest of this book by doing three things. The first was embedding research in a wider philosophical framework on the nature of science. Social science is a debate, which revolves around solving puzzles, and which is based on the idea that theories and facts are caught in a three-cornered fight. Relevant data both falsify an existing theory and allow for the development of a new theory. Research design is the practical manifestation of these philosophical insights in the way we conduct social science: it provides logical links between question, debate, working hypothesis, and data so that you can turn plausible ideas into convincing arguments. Since sound research questions are, in this view, the key to sound research, I discussed the basic criteria that research questions have to meet to find an easy place in the architecture of sophisticated falsificationism.

The central idea that ran through the discussion in this chapter was that, contrary to what we are often told, we construct our understanding of the social and political world ('social science') ourselves: your construction of the debate, your argument, and your construction of data form the foundations of research. The world is not objectively given, waiting to be discovered, and neither is the literature; you need to construct a viable question, an intelligent debate that you want to be a part of, and link that to the arguments you build and the data you collect. But since it has this strong subjective moment, we need principles that guide us. Combined, these principles are what we call research design.

The next chapters of this book deal with the practical implications of these discussions and insights. In the next chapter, we will explore four methodological dimensions of research which logically precede research design, in order to allow you better to think about the nature of relevant data and how they can be linked to questions and arguments. Chapter 3 goes through the main non-statistical methods used in the social sciences today: case studies and systematic comparative research. Chapter 4 will discuss the nature of data (both qualitative and quantitative), how to construct them, and how to use them. In Chapter 5, the focus shifts from producing research to reproducing research: how to write a report on your research that brings out all its good qualities. The Appendix, finally, is a guide to the profession: how to present and criticize papers, and how to write good research proposals. The concluding chapter will tie some of these different threads together and send you off with a health warning.

FURTHER READING TO INTRODUCTION AND CHAPTER 1

It still pays to read the classics. Durkheim's *Suicide* and Weber's *Protestant Ethic and the Spirit of Capitalism* remain benchmarks for any starting researcher. Marvel at their (often implicit) research design, thought through, remember, long before we spent much time on these things. Read them side by side and discover how different their approaches to the world are.

The Popper–Kuhn–Lakatos debate is best read through the original texts. I found *Conjectures and Refutations* (Popper 1989, original edition 1963), especially chapter 1, easier to digest than the *Logic of Scientific Discovery* (Popper 1959). Kuhn's *Structure of Scientific Revolutions* (1962) is his famous statement of the development of science. And Lakatos was, I found, best approached through the dense but exceedingly rich 'Falsification and the Methodology of Scientific Research Programmes' (Lakatos 1970), in which he explicitly engages Kuhn and Popper. This latter text is not easy-reading and may take you a few hours to complete, but it's time well-spent. If a good teacher helps you explore it in a seminar, and unpacks its implications for what you are starting off on, you will find that the insights in the text are very helpful for the rest of your life.

There is now a small library on research design *stricto sensu*. King et al. (1994) is perhaps not always fun to read, but a good benchmark. Brady and Collier (2004) present the debate that King et al. started, and with it revamped the entire field of qualitative research methods.

2 Constructing a Research Design

Most, possibly all, graduate programmes in the social sciences today require students to take a basic inferential statistics class, where they learn how regression coefficients are constructed, what the meaning of significance levels is, and some general rules about how to handle (usually interpret rather than perform) regression analysis. This is generally a good thing: if a large part of your discipline relies on sophisticated statistical analysis, knowing how to read such articles is a crucial skill. But there is a problem: too often, the research skills training in graduate programmes stops there, and other research designs are treated as the weak little brother of statistical analysis.

This methodological snobbery has had several unfortunate consequences. The first is that, after a few classes in regression analysis, students start throwing statistics at every problem that has numbers associated with them. The statistical packages SPSS and STATA now run on most laptops and with such low practical thresholds, there is a proliferation of quantitative work. Regression analysis, however, is only one of a wide variety of quantitative techniques, and often not even the best one for a particular problem. Cluster analysis or factor analysis, for example, work on the assumption that cases or variables are closely linked instead of (statistically) independent. The second is that other research designs, which deal with non-numerical information, are often treated very cursorily in graduate training programmes, without much critical sense of either their strengths or their weaknesses. The third is that while the people who 'do' case studies are not quite treated as second-class citizens anymore in the relevant discipline, their contributions are often treated as interesting rather than conclusive: 'if the argument is that good, prove it with statistics', seems to be the general motto. What many ignore, or forget if they knew, is that statistics is, as a data-handling technique, especially good at dealing with research questions of a particular type, while so-called qualitative research (or 'configurational' research) appears better at handling other kinds of questions. This chapter therefore starts by unpacking when to do what: are there good reasons why researchers would rely on statistics as opposed to case studies and vice versa? (Since many terms that are common in thinking about statistics appear throughout this chapter, the glossary in Table 2.1 gives intuitive definitions of the most crucial ones for the—slightly anxious—uninitiated reader).

After drawing that balance sheet which, I hope, will allow beginning researchers to think about their methods in a more sophisticated way, the chapter continues with a basic but often ignored dimension of empirical research in much of the social sciences: the nature of the universe that you are working on. Before you start your research, the idea is, you have to know where what you study is located in relation to the rest of the world. The final section deals with the elephant in the room of the social sciences: time and history. Since all the processes we study take place over time, we need to acknowledge that. However, few of our methods actually know how to account for time; most techniques we have, in fact, suspend time. In statistics, for example, we are looking for 'time-less' universal relationships and assume that having a large enough sample allows us to capture the possible variation that might exist over time. A short final section wraps up these preliminary thoughts and sets the stage for Chapter 3.

Variables, cases, and configurations

Imagine you had access to data on a very large number of people, and wanted to find out the effect of an improvement in living conditions on such things as general health and longevity. You could try to reconstruct a small number of individual biographies that included the jobs people held, the cities where they lived, and the housing space they had available, see at which point in their lives diets improved or worsened, and where that led in terms of health and life expectancy. But that would be a very cumbersome and time-consuming task, unlikely to yield few robust insights: you would never be certain that you captured the relevant issues despite your painstakingly detailed work, and even if you were, you would

Table 2.1 Stats for non-quants

Note: This glossary gives a series of intuitive definitions of commonly used statistical terms in this chapter for readers who are unfamiliar with them. Quantitatively trained readers can skip this table without missing anything important.

Measuring 'averages' There are three ways to measure what is *commonly called the average in a population.* Example: imagine a group of four people from small to tall—A is 166 cm in height, B 170 cm, C 170 cm, and D 190 cm—as the sample we are interested in.	The *mean* is the sum of all values on a variable, divided by the number of observations. In the example above, the mean height is $(166 + 170 + 170 + 190)/4 = 174$ cm. The mean income in a country is the total income of a country divided by the population. The *median* is the value where, after the observations are ranked from low to high, there are exactly 50% of the observations on both sides. In the example above, the median is 170 cm. In the case of an odd number of observations, the median is one observation. If there are an even number of observations, there are two middle numbers and the median is the mean of these two. When political scientists talk about the median voter, they refer to the voter who controls the vote at exactly 50% of the population, that is, the voter who, in a two-party system, will grant a majority to one party. If the parties are interested in obtaining a majority of the votes, this voter's preferences are likely to be very well reflected in party platforms and possibly policies.
Mean, median, and mode can be the same or very different, depending on the distribution of variables.	The *mode* is the value which appears most frequently, in the example the mode is 170. When political scientists and economists talk about 'modal income', they usually refer to the income bracket which contains most of the population.
Distributions	Values can be very differently distributed across populations. A normal distribution means that there are more or less as many observations on both sides of the mean, with the extreme values on both sides roughly equally far apart from the mean—a bell-shaped curve around the mean. But a distribution can be, as in the example above, left-skewed (or right-skewed, if there are more variables on the right-hand side of the mean). Most standard statistics rely on the assumption of a normal distribution. Distributions can be identified everywhere, but really only matter in statistics for large enough populations or samples (30 is considered the minimum number of observations for statistics to be useful). This is referred to in the text as 'large-N'; population numbers below 30 are referred to as 'small-N' (usually considered between 1 and 5) and 'medium-N' (up until 30).

(cont.)

Table 2.1 (*Continued*)

Standard deviations	Once we know the mean of a sample, we can find out how well the mean represents that population. The standard deviation (SD) gives a sense of the extent to which individual observations deviate from the mean. A population with the values 2, 10, and 15 and one with the values 8, 9, and 10 give a mean of (27/3=) 9. However, the second distribution has a much smaller SD than the first, since the individual values 8, 9, and 10 are much closer to the mean which is 9.
Statistical independence	Statistical analysis requires that the value of one observation should not influence the value on another observation. This is called 'independence'. In the example of heights above, the measurements are almost certainly independent: A's height has little influence on B's height, etc. Daily weather patterns are not independent: today's weather is influenced by yesterday's. Similarly, growth rates or electoral returns are almost always influenced by what happened to the economy the previous year or to the electoral results in the previous election.
Regression coefficients	Regression coefficients report, in condensed form, how a change in the value of one or a number of variables affects the value for another variable. These values 'predict', in other words, how the variable that you are interested in will vary as a result of these changes in independent variables. If a set of variables predicts an outcome very well, the coverage of the variance (or R^2), which varies between 0 and 1 with 1 being the highest score, is high. Predicted values are (almost) always different from actual values.
Standard errors	Standard errors give a sense of the extent to which individual observations deviate from the values that the regression analysis predicts. They are also used for analysis of means of samples (standard error of the mean, or SEM), in the same way standard deviations are used in analysis of means for a population.
Significance levels	Statistics is based on probability. Significance levels report to what extent the data sample with which you are working reflects the underlying population, that is, how high the probability is that what you find in your data actually reflects correlations in the wider population that you are interested in and are not just a random outcome. Generally 90%, 95%, and 99% are the significance levels where one can safely make claims about the population on the basis of the statistical or regression outcomes from the sample.
Statistical controls	We might have a fairly good idea of other variables beyond the ones that we are interested in which may affect the value of the dependent variable. We introduce those other variables as 'controls'. In effect, we keep those variables constant and then see what has happened to the strength and direction of the relationship of the variable we are interested in.

Degrees of freedom

Degrees of freedom are best understood as the number of observations or cases in your sample minus the number of variables. In order to perform a meaningful statistical analysis, the number of variables has to be smaller than the number of cases. The reason is simply that, if this is not the case, many equations can be written for your regression which would all technically be correct.

Dummy variables

Some variables take categorical values, such as 1 or 0, or can be constructed as having such values (belonging to EMU, being Germany, when Barack Obama was president, etc.). Assessing the effects of such categorical values is done with dummy variables. If we have a dummy variable that is binary (i.e. yes or no, present or not present) it is coded as 1 for yes or 0 for no in the statistical analysis.

Lagged variables

Some variables may have effects, say, one or two years later. Economic growth today may have effects on inflation next year or the year after, for example. Lagged variables are introduced to handle that: inflation in 2001 is regressed against economic growth for 2000.

Interaction terms

If you think that the effect you are interested in only or mainly occurs when two processes simultaneously push towards it, you examine interaction terms that distil the combined effect of these two processes. You construct, as it were, a virtual variable that measures this joint effect.

not know if your small sample allowed you to say anything about those people that were not lucky enough to find themselves in it. The standard way to handle such a question is through statistics: as a doctor who examines recruits for military service, for example, you have access to basic data of several hundreds of thousands of young men over time, and the question you are asking allows itself to be expressed in a few numbers that (are assumed to) capture the dimensions which are relevant for your question. Run just a few basic correlations between parents' income and jobs, diet, and some crude indicator of standard of living, on the one hand, and general health and life expectancy on the other, and compare those over time—in, say, ten-year intervals between 1950 and 2000—and you have your answer. (Note that some medical studies are forced to rely on the quasi-biographical method described above: if a condition is so rare that only five people in a few million are afflicted by it, and if you take into account that the developed (OECD) world only counts about 1 billion people and that not everyone lives long enough for the disease to manifest itself, you will find that you have only ten, or perhaps twenty, cases to draw on. Faced with those methodological constraints, qualitative research is often the only way to find out what the causes and effects of these diseases are—Oliver Sacks has made a career of analysing such almost unique cases; see Sacks [1986].)

Why is the use of statistics such a powerful tool to examine this question? The first reason is that you can slice the information into small bits called variables and capture most of the relevant information in a few indicators: height, weight, and general health, for example, are easy to measure, and are good joint measures of the things you are interested in. The same information can also be acquired through long interviews, but while you obviously would know a lot more after that, it is unclear how much more *relevant* information you would obtain. Secondly, your question is asked in terms of quite narrow marginal changes and effects: you try to find out how a change (improvement) in the diet affects a change (improvement) in life expectancy. You are not all that interested in how life expectancy is affected by everything good or bad that happens in a person's life. Thirdly, you have access to a large number of observations, which allows you to filter out irrelevant variation such as climate, marital status, etc. And finally, you can use the sample of young army recruits as a window onto the larger population—in fact, as women are recruited in armies as well since the 1960s, you have a chance of checking for gender bias.

Now imagine that you are interested in a very different question: over history, you have noticed, some countries become democratic and remain stable democracies, while others seem to revert to dictatorship after a few years as a functioning democracy (interwar Italy and Weimar Germany as examples of the latter), and you want to find out why. This is a big question, but not a big world to study: even after 1989, the number of possibly relevant cases is not much more than a few dozen (including Latin America and Central Europe). Moreover, the types of answers you want to explore will almost certainly encompass complex combinations of causes. In the case of Germany, for example, what matters are such events and processes as the First World War and the Versailles Treaty, the dynamics of the polarizing party system and the struggles between social-democratic and communist parties, the rapidly changing class structure, the rise of the Nazi party from very humble beginnings, etc. The conditions under which consolidation happened or did not happen are very different across all the possible cases as well: the First World War and its aftermath may help to understand Italy and Germany, but is at best a very distant cause for any other country that you would be interested in.

This type of question requires, because of the complexity of the possible answers, the potential uniqueness of each case and the possibility of more than one way for democracy to collapse and/or to be consolidated, that you explore and unpack individual cases. In a way you have to abandon the ideas of random variation and generalizability at the basis of statistics altogether, and produce 'biographies' of countries or compare a very small number of them—usually not more than a handful (Moore [1967] and Skocpol [1979] are classic examples of such comparative analyses). And these analyses will almost certainly receive a lot of their power from emphasizing the idiosyncratic elements of each case, not from pointing out what they share and use that as a basis for generalization. Like an amateur historian you will have to rely on secondary and under-explored primary sources to map the causal mechanisms and analyse them in a 'thick' way, paying a lot of attention to detail and subtle links. Since your ability to grasp the complexities of many different cases is limited, especially as a beginning researcher (things get better as you get older, so this might be a project to finish rather than start your career with), you will be lucky if you can say anything meaningful about more than two, three, or perhaps four countries.

Both these questions address highly important problems. The effect of changes in living standards on life expectancy and the conditions under which democracies consolidate make up, in some form or other, a large part of the libraries in political and economic history, political economy, political science, and sociology. The remarkable thing, though, is that the way you would do research on one tells us very little about how to do research on the other. The reason is quite simple: the methodological conditions under which the research takes place differ tremendously between the two cases. In the first case, you can ignore the individual cases (the army recruits) and concentrate on the variables that you extracted from them. You can then assess the impact of changes in one variable in light of changes in other variables. And since you have enough recruits to work with, you can introduce multiple correlations, statistical controls, and interaction terms to check for spurious correlations and joint effects. In the case of democracy studies, in contrast, you are interested in understanding a very small number of specific outcomes that are both very singular and highly contingent. Rewinding the film of Weimar Germany, for example, adding one ingredient such as cooperation between the Communist and the Social-Democratic Parties, and playing it again might, as Steven Jay Gould (1990) said about life on Earth, well yield a different outcome with less atrocious consequences for the continent. The integrity of the cases is crucial, in other words. Turning them into variables that are 'independent' of one another probably undermines the entire idea for your project: the First World War and Versailles are perhaps not like any other war and peace treaty in the past, and what you are interested in are the precise outcomes and the precise causes of the collapse of democracy in Italy and Germany, not some general abstract regularity. Imagine, for example, that you tried a statistical analysis and therefore had to score the First World War against the Second World War: which one would receive a 4 on your 5-point scale, and why? What would such a scale really measure anyway? Even if you managed to turn the complex cases into variables, you would still be stuck with a universe that is too small to do systematic statistical research. And assuming that you can jump over that hurdle, there is a deep methodological issue which statistical analysis cannot resolve: your initial guess was, quite reasonably, that the actual effect of the First World War and Versailles, taken separately, only mattered against the background of a fragmenting party system, and a resurgent, and particularly nasty, form of German nationalism in the context of a polarizing class structure.

Large-N statistical analysis and small-N configurational analysis are very different methods (Ragin 1987; Kittel 2006; Shalev 2007), which force you to ask different questions (or conversely lend themselves to answering very different questions), and which might lead to very different answers as well (Rueschemeyer et al. 1991). They differ along four key lines (summarized in Table 2.2). Statistical analysis looks for *marginal* causes and effects, holding constant other possible explanations. It tries to assess the impact of one or a small number of variables on an outcome of interest—for example, how parents' income and jobs influence the chances of their offspring acquiring higher education. It relies on *variables* which are *independent* of each other: the value on one observation is not influenced by other observations. And it is *additive* in the sense that it estimates the marginal effect of a variable in light of a few others (maximize your R^2 with as few variables as possible and estimate their individual contributions). You try to find out how the income of parents has an effect, first, and then you add to that the possible independent effect of the jobs they held on the likelihood that their son or daughter will go to university.

Configurational analysis, in contrast, relies on explanations that are of a '*discrete*' nature (think back to the example of the collapse of democracy earlier for this discussion): it sees cases as indivisible units that hang together in systemic ways. The mode of analysis is *configurational* in the sense that a particular combination of factors contributes to a particular outcome. And its basic method is (for want of a better term) '*subtractive*', identifying necessary and sufficient conditions (or combinations of these) under which a particular outcome occurred. The answers you can obtain

Table 2.2 Statistical and configurational analysis compared

	Statistical analysis	Configurational analysis
Type of explanation	Marginal effects	'Holistic'
Unit of observation	Variables	Cases as discrete units
Method of answering	Additive	'Subtractive'
Type of answers	General	Specific

are very different as well. Statistical analysis has the ambition to *generalize* from the sample to the population at large. Configurational analysis identifies specific causalities which, if the same conditions are present, will hold for similarly organized cases. Sometimes bridges exist between the two: interaction terms in statistical analysis, for example, are based on the idea that several factors simultaneously can have an effect—but the problem, as everyone familiar with statistics knows, is that you need a very large sample, and a more or less normal distribution within that sample, to avoid running out of degrees of freedom. On the whole, though, these two broad research designs are part of different methodo-logical families.

If indeed these two broad approaches are members of different families, then the choice between them is not just given by the number of potential observations that you can work with, but primarily by the type of question you ask: if you want to know why something happened, you are trying to use your analytical powers to make sense of a complex historical issue, and you are willing to sacrifice parsimony for that (cf. Bronk [2009: 281–4] for a similar distinction). Take the Holocaust. It was not 'caused' by a par-ticular alignment of important factions of business with the Nazis (see the debate between Abraham [1981] and Turner [1985]), nor by a particularly deep-seated anti-semitism that Germans had carried over in different forms for the last three centuries (Goldhagen 1996), nor by the irrational fears of the middle classes who voted the Nazis in power (see Hamilton [1996] for a critical treatment of this proposition), or by the nationalism that emerged out of the treatment that Germany received in the Versailles Treaty. All of these factors may have mattered in some form or other in the case of Germany, and therefore none of them could lay claim to being the 'ultimate' cause. If however, you are interested in why such mass genocides happen—in Nazi Germany, in Armenia, in Rwanda, in the Balkans, etc.— then you want to find out which characteristics these cases share. In such an endeavour, an approach that allows you to abstract from the specifics of the German Holocaust is necessary (the Versailles Treaty explanation, as well as the specific version of German anti-semitism, thus may well disappear from the set of useful explanations).

One final implication for starting researchers sheds a critical light on a prevailing fashion in the social sciences. Students are often told to check their results for robustness through methodological 'triangulation': if a causal claim emerges using case studies, they are told, then check if it also holds using, for instance, some form of statistical analysis or *vice versa*. This can be an excellent idea: since statistical analysis and configurational analysis have systematic and often complementary strengths and weaknesses, they will compensate for those and thus make your findings more robust. You could even imagine isolating causal sub-claims of complex arguments that you test statistically on broader populations, or of 'nesting' a case-based analysis within a statistical study to examine rival theories (Lieberman 2005). However, this strategy of combining methods is subject to one crucial background condition: it assumes that the question allows itself to be answered with different methods. That might be the case, but is not necessarily so. If large-N statistics-based analysis and small-N configurational analysis are indeed ways to answer fundamentally different questions, as I suggested earlier (and if a translation from one into the other is impossible, for methodological or more pragmatic data availability reasons), there is, in principle, no bridge between the two, and triangulation makes little sense. In those instances, the morale is clear: stick with one method, and do it superbly.[1]

Now that we have this baseline model for selecting approaches and methods, let us move on to the nature of empirical material. Two issues are useful to discuss. The next section deals with the crucial issue of the

---

[1] There is, in fact, a stronger methodological argument against mixing methods, which Carsten Schneider explained to me and for which I owe him my gratitude. Imagine a population of, say thirty-five cases of genocide. About half of them lie on or very close to the regression line. Mixed-methods thinking suggests to take any case on the regression line as 'typical', and then use what happened there as a way of understanding 'all' the other cases. But this has serious problems: the fit on the regression line is determined as much by the simultaneous presence of conditions for genocide and its actual occurrence in those instances (present, present) as it is determined by the joint absence of necessary conditions for genocide and genocide as such. A good regression fit can, in the limiting case, be obtained with only a single case where both the conditions and the outcome are present— as long as not too many others logically contradict that combination! The upshot is that there are therefore, *within* the regression analysis itself, no useful ways to decide if a case is 'typical' or not, and such mixed-methods analyses may end up being misleading rather than enlightening (Rohlfing 2008). Always check your data with simpler methods than complicated statistics to see if they make intuitive sense.

definition of a relevant universe, while the final one introduces time as a factor in the social and political world.

Observations and the relevant universe

Research always has the ambition to say something about a wider universe, because we either have a representative sample on which we perform strong statistical techniques, draw far-reaching conclusions on the basis of the individual case we study, or are convinced that the causal mechanisms we identified help us understand other cases that we did not study. Developing a good sense of the relevant universe of your study is a crucial step before any analysis of data, whatever the nature of these data. The world is a big place, and most of the time we cannot study every instance of a causal mechanism that we might be interested in. While statistical analysis resolves that problem by associating probabilities to samples, configurational research designs cannot rely on large numbers and random sampling, often because the data do not present themselves in a way that allows us to do so, or because the question we ask cannot be captured in the standard probabilistic terms of statistical analysis. It is therefore especially in the latter case that a good sense of the relevant universe matters.

Defining your relevant universe can take several forms, but at the very least it should tell an outsider how your observations (data or cases) allow you to shed light on a broader question. Think of the following questions as ways of ascertaining that. Are the data randomly selected or not? If not, what were the criteria for selection? Is the case you are studying a typical case, an outlier on the left-hand side of the distribution of the cases that are relevant for you (a very likely instance, let's say) or on the right-hand side (very unlikely)? If you think it is a typical case, how can you demonstrate that without relying on a 'trust me' argument? What does this say about cases that are not 'typical'? And is the distribution such that the typical case you have identified (say, an average or modal case) also coincides more or less with the median case which has roughly equal numbers of cases on both sides? Without some information on these questions, a case is and remains a single data point with few other implications than informed speculation.

Take the following example. A few years ago, I reviewed a paper which performed quite a sophisticated statistical analysis of change in an industry in Germany, but failed to explain why that industry was a particularly suitable place to study these processes. The author responded to my comments by including more significance tests. What I asked was, in my mind, a relatively simple but important question: what do insights on that particular industry tell us about similar processes in other industries? Are they likely to be the same, very different, or even the opposite of what the author claimed? Significance tests do not answer that question.

The general problem of the relevant universe can be broken down into several dimensions. One of the first things is to think deeply about the nature of the data you are gathering. Many of us, infused with a statistical bias, go for collecting as many data as possible, on the assumption that if a causal mechanism holds for five instead of two cases, it is more valid (King et al. 1994: 24). More instances that can be explained is certainly better than fewer; the question is, however, if that is not something better to explore after you have finished the research rather than before. Your case will, in a statistical sense, never be representative, even if you think it is a typical case, and criteria borrowed from statistics may therefore be misleading. However, since you selected cases and universe in light of the question you are asking and the type of answer you want to give, you can use the way you have set up your question as a tool to help you find out which cases to select and which ones to ignore (much more on that in the next chapter). Make sure, though, that you make explicit which criteria you relied on to select observations: in addition to being able to improve on the research design through comments from supervisors and colleagues if the cases are weak, it also allows others to disagree with you. If you make explicit how you selected cases, they then have to argue explicitly with you why they disagree with your criteria and what would be better ones for case selection.

Your universe needs to be defined so that it has a logical ending. If a question has to be closed at the front and the end, as I argued in the previous chapter, your observations have to follow that rule symmetrically. That means that you have to think about such issues as the period you study—why that particular beginning and ending?—and the geographic areas you treat as relevant. As a student in European Studies, for example, it might seem logical to study contemporary 'Europe'. But be aware that it really is not: many people are not interested in 'Europe' *per se*. Show that there is a broader issue that you can tackle through a study of something that is happening in Europe today. Since geography is no longer necessarily destiny, delimitations in space need a better explanation than so-called intrinsic relevance.

One of the standard ways of closing a research question is by stating that your data included the last year for which observations were available. Whilst this sounds reasonable, it is not generally a good way to close your research. A colleague of mine told me the story of a paper he had submitted to a top journal in economics. The paper examined the transition in several Central European countries over the period 1990–2005, the last year for which data could be found, and was probably as strong as such papers were ever going to get: it had a clear model, a strong regression analysis, up-to-date empirical data, and interesting findings and conclusion. Despite that, one reviewer rejected it on the basis that there were insufficient observations. 'What am I supposed to do?' my friend exclaimed, 'Tear down the Berlin Wall a few years earlier?' When your data are limited as these were, the onus is on you to argue that the period you study is a logically closed unit. When you do this, make sure that any such periodization also corresponds to a more general intersubjective interpretation of the period. Armed with World Bank statistics, you could suggest, for example, that by 2005, something had come to a close in Central Europe: the rate of change of structural adjustment had slowed to a 'normal' (compared to OECD economies) rate, economic policy had become slow-moving and continuous by then, or that big shifts in economic policy from the early 1990s have had the time to work their way through the system, which means that we can treat the period as closed.

The third dimension is to check your cases for *comparability*. How do you know that A and B are comparable? Many years ago, when I was a graduate student, someone explained in a job interview how he compared Belgian provinces, German *Länder* (member-states) and French *régions* to understand some policy. While all are indeed sub-national political units, they are far from comparable: provinces in Belgium have an almost cosmetic function without any real power associated with them, and while French *régions* could be construed as having more autonomy, they were nothing in comparison to German *Länder*, who have a lot of autonomy, up to the possibility of blocking laws that were voted in the federal-level lower house (Bundestag). In terms of actual political role, the German *Länder* came out on top because of their veto power, followed by the considerably weaker French *régions*, and finally by the almost irrelevant Belgian provinces. Comparing them as if they are similar is deeply misleading.

In an enlightening article, Locke and Thelen (1995) argue that comparability implies that you sometimes explicitly have to compare two different things, because those that look the same may play a different role in different settings and *vice versa*. Working time, as they point out, is a politically highly salient issue in Germany, but not at all in the United States, because of how the labour unions have politicized it in one country but not in the other. Conversely, job classifications are the core of labour politics in the United States and not at all in Germany: the labour unions in the United States were built upon the rule of clear job classifications and occupational demarcations, whereas in Germany workplace institutions that represent workers are trusted by all and job demarcations do not matter nearly as much. They argue that we should compare issues with the same salience in different countries, so that apples (but which may be disguised as oranges) are compared with other apples.

One of the final things to keep in mind is to think through *how many dimensions* the relevant universe has. If the outcome you are interested in can be meaningfully understood along one dimension, then two cases are both necessary and sufficient for your analysis. If, however, your argument involves more than one dimension, and you can capture each of these in dichotomous terms, you are looking at a minimum of four (2×2) cases to answer the question you are asking. The number of necessary cases rises exponentially with the number of dimensions as the exponent: the formula is 2^x, where 'x' stands for the number of dimensions. Sometimes forcing yourself to do this, may even open up interesting new dimensions to your initial question.

Take the different modes of privatization in the former Soviet Union and Central Europe as an example. When you compare Russia and the Visegrad-4 countries (V4: Czech Republic, Hungary, Poland, and Slovakia), you realize that privatization in Russia often followed an 'insider' model in which assets were sold to existing management and workers, and an outsider model in the V4, where companies were sold or handed over to the population at large or to foreign investors (King 2007). You then claim that companies in the second case perform better: foreign owners import new organization and technology, and care about profit instead of high wages and stable jobs. A glance at Slovenia, however, suggests that this is probably not correct: Slovenian companies were sold to insiders, yet they perform very well. Introducing a second dimension—something along the lines of 'was decision-making in the pre-capitalist political economy highly centralized or highly decentralized?'—you can resolve the problem that you found a well-performing case of insider privatiza- tion. In Slovenia, as in other pre-1991 Yugoslav republics, local workers' councils played a large role in company management. In Russia, in contrast, many microeconomic decisions were made centrally. Insider privatization, you could argue, fell on very different soil in the two instances, with different consequences. Your problem may be resolved, but you now have a new one, since you have three cases and implicitly two dimensions along which you selected cases: insider/outsider mode of privatization and centralized/decentralized pre-capitalist political econ- omy. Make these dimensions explicit, and think through what your universe looks like now (see Table 2.3), and where interesting cases lie within that.

You can use this insight on the number of dimensions in your universe the other way around. Students often start thinking about their research project in terms of three cases, usually based on the idea that three is more than two and therefore yields more generalizable outcomes, but not as much as four, which is too much work. Correct, but slightly irrelevant. If you find yourself with three cases, apply the one-or-two-dimensions rule. (If more than two relevant dimensions appear as the way to conceptualize your universe, think hard: eight detailed case studies is a lot of work.) If you can capture your research object in one dimension, two well-chosen

Table 2.3 Modes of privatization and political economy (hypothesis)

	Mode of privatization	
	Insider	Outsider
Nature of pre-capitalist political economy		
Centralized	Patrimonial capitalism Russia 1990s	Dependent liberal capitalism Visegrad-4 1990s
Decentralized	Corporatist capitalism Slovenia 1990s	Liberal capitalism OECD, esp. UK/US 1980–2008

cases are enough; if the world comes in two dimensions, you need at least four cases. Three is, in other words, usually either one too many (in which case you can save yourself the trouble and not waste six months of your life) or one short of what you need. The extra information you may think you gain through the third case is a mirage: you want to make an argument, not describe the world, and arguments require logic, not numbers. However, once you managed to make your point in its crispiest form with just two cases and established the relevant causalities and mechanisms, you could (and probably should) revisit other cases to see if and how your argument travels to parallel instances and use that material to shed additional light on the argument you are making— when it works and when it does not. This is the moment where you leave the parsimonious and crisp two-case research design and generalize your insights relying on less clear-cut cases. An example: if you find that cooperative labour relations helped the German car industry in the 1980s adjust better than the adversarial labour relations in the United States allowed the Big Three, you can then deploy the arguments in that narrow and crisp comparison of the automotive sector to examine what happened in that industry in other countries (Sweden and the United Kingdom, e.g., with similar differences), or in other industries in Germany and the United States (Turner 1991).

So far, in a way, so bad. We now know that we cannot always rely on strong statistical techniques: the data may not be good enough or, more importantly, the question is not asked in a way where statistical analysis makes a lot of sense. We have also discovered that we have to be very self-aware with regard to the way our universe is structured. Let us now add a third complication: time and history.

Time and history in the social sciences

All social and political events take place in history. Most of the standard ways of analysing social and political phenomena do not really give us tools to deal with that, since they unfortunately assume some form of 'time-lessness'. Schmitter (2008) therefore quite rightly argues that carefully constructed narratives remain key in understanding processes that have a strong temporal dimension. Paul Pierson (2004) devoted a whole book to these methodological problems of time in social science, in fact, which I strongly recommend to beginning researchers; most of the points below also appear in Pierson's book and are treated in significantly more detail there. From those discussions, I have distilled five key points to consider when building a research design that allude to time: sequence, timing, context, asymmetry, and change.

Sequence. Does it matter that B takes place after A? The first thing to keep in mind here is that sequence matters in terms of causality: A can cause B only if it precedes B. A simple, but often forgotten point when scholars mistake causal for functional arguments in which the existence of B increases the likelihood that A, which chronologically precedes B, exists or survives. Such functionalist explanations are not so much wrong as over-stretching their causal range. For example, you could argue that works' councils in Germany, which incorporate the voice of workers in the management of the company, easily persist despite the fact that they impose adjustment costs in difficult times, by referring to the beneficial effect they have of allowing companies to find more as well as more peaceful adjustment paths. This may be true, but since the effect of works councils follows their existence, it is not really a causal argument. A causal argument would require that you also demonstrate that German employers, when faced with problems, rely on works councils for corporate restructuring, and therefore include that in their calculation at times when they could reduce the powers of works' councils (Wood 2001).

There is a second, more complicated issue associated with sequence. If we think of a problem, and we think of it in terms of a set of necessary conditions, we sometimes ignore the possibility that these conditions have to appear in a particular sequence for the outcome that we are interested in to be produced. In other words, we need to think not only in terms of the collection of conditions, but also in terms of their mutual interrelation in time. It matters, for example, that property rights are clearly established and that they are constitutionally enshrined *before* vast amounts of assets are privatized (Stiglitz 1999). In Central Europe, governments got that more or less right. But in places such as Russia, privatizations often happened before property rights were clear, and the effect has been an oligarchic outcome, in which party apparatchiks control companies which are private in name rather than substance. Introducing policies in the correct sequence, as Stiglitz (1999) suggested, is therefore as important as the substance of the policies themselves.

Timing. Does it matter when something takes place? The same event may have different effects, depending on when it happens. That was one of the issues at the core of dependency theory's critique of modernization: industrializing in the nineteenth century is a very different thing from doing so in the twentieth century, because the world economy looks very different in 1960 than it did in 1860, and late developers have to play by rules established by early industrializers. Closer to home: consider the 1960s–1970s and the 1990s, and compare the introduction of democratic capitalism in Spain and Portugal in the 1970s with the same process in Central Europe (the idea for this comparison was handed to me by my colleague Abby Innes). In the 1970s, the prevailing idea in political economy was that the state could play an important role in steering economic activities. In the southern European countries the transition to democratic capitalism thus took the shape of a dramatic extension of state activities in the economy, in part to compensate for existing inefficiencies in the economic system, and in part to legitimize the transition in the eyes of the potentially many losers. By the early 1990s, after Reagan's famous phrase (as much a conservative diagnosis as a programmatic statement) that 'government is the problem, not the solution', which heralded a very different conception of the role of the state in the economy, political–economic transitions into capitalism were bound to adopt a different logic.

Standard methods in social science almost completely ignore this problem. If data are available, social scientists usually rely on 'pooled time series', the technique by which observations over different years are pooled into one data-set, sometimes a lagged variable is introduced, and then standard statistical analysis is performed on that new data-set. But such pooled time series analysis is often a very bad idea. Many variables, such as constitutions, electoral systems, size of government, and modes of decision-making in non-parliamentary channels, do not vary all that much over time within one country. Researchers thus throw fast-moving variables such as GDP growth, inflation, or productivity growth in a regression with very slow-moving variables such as government composition, or medium-term invariants such as electoral systems or wage-bargaining systems. The other reason is that you have in effect taken history out of the analysis: a one- or two-year lag still assumes substantive continuity in the data. Medium- and long-term shifts, for example the shift in GDP or employment from industry to services, the growing economic and political participation of women, or the rise of new policy paradigms, all processes which usually play out over several decades, are simply ignored.

Take the relation between government spending and unemployment. If you run a pooled regression for the period 1970–2000, you will very likely find no significant correlation between fiscal policy and unemployment: in the 1970s, the relation was strong; in the 1980s, it fell to at best moderately strong; and in the 1990s, it may have disappeared altogether in most OECD countries. But split the data in two periods, say 1970–84 and 1985–2000, thus distinguishing between a period when Keynesianism was still the dominant macro-economic policy paradigm, and one when monetarism was dominant, and you are likely to find, in fact, two very strong correlations but with different signs. One of the reasons is that after 1985, monetary stability, with or without independent central banks, rather than full employment, became the explicit goal of government policy. Rises in government spending were immediately treated as suspicious because they were potentially inflationary and therefore counter-acted through restrictive monetary policy which led to higher unemployment. Aware of this new constraint, governments thus adopted more conservative fiscal stances, which contributed to low growth. A less sophisticated but better way to handle this is to introduce these shifts into the analysis, in the same way that a historian would split up his or her world in periods, compare averages for the period, and then see if a statistical model, with dummies for the two periods, still makes sense.

Context. Do large-scale universals such as technological development or shifts in the international system matter for your analysis? Take the internet—possibly the most important technological shock of the last two decades and so ubiquitous that we now write it in lowercase as if it is a generic noun. Being a dictator in the 1970s or 1980s was, if you could ignore the questionable moral dimension of your job, relatively easy. All you needed was a large and loyal army and police force, a muzzled press, and a secret police organization or a few death squads to identify and neutralize opponents to your rule. Running a decent dictatorship today is considerably harder. Even if you still have the army, police forces, and death squads, it is much more difficult to control the flow of information in and out of the country. Even the quite formidable Chinese communist party, for example, has had to rely on Google's ability to block internet sites and breach basic privacy rights in order to control the flow of information within the country. The last few decades have seen quite a few of such sudden shocks: the World Wide Web, of course, but think also of the collapse of the bipolar world with the fall of the Soviet empire, the institution of EMU in Europe, or the wars in Iraq and the subsequent destabilization of the Middle East. Whatever your question, sit back and ask if, for what you are trying to understand, it matters that the world seems to have changed in a big way. If it does not, fine; if it does, build it in as part of your research. But do not ignore it.

Asymmetry. Was something a necessary condition for the growth of a phenomenon, but played no role in the decline of that phenomenon? Such asymmetries may indeed be important, but the conventional ways of thinking in the social sciences do not always know how to handle them very well. If a rise in X caused an increase in Y, then it is quite sensible to think that a fall in X is likely to cause a drop in Y. In many instances where we do research, this may undoubtedly be a plausible assumption. In some, however, it may not be and discovering this is often a good start for developing research questions which exploit such asymmetries. You may inadvertently be onto something considerably more interesting than you thought at the start. Take the growth and retrenchment of the welfare state as an example (Pierson 2004). Assume that the welfare state grew as a result of how organized labour and social-democratic parties used their power in the post-war era to make workers less dependent on market income (Korpi 1983; Esping-Andersen 1990). With the shift in the balance of political power from labour to business and away from social-democratic ideas over the last three decades, a plausible prediction would be that welfare spending will be reduced. If this were the case, then the United States under Reagan and Bush Sr. or the United Kingdom under Thatcher would be among the first places where you could witness such a retrenchment: organized labour was eliminated from the political scene, and for over a decade conservative parties advocating neo-liberal economic and welfare policies were in office in those countries. But Pierson demonstrated that retrenchment follows a very different logic from growth, since a growing welfare state produces its own supporting coalitions, which make cuts for those groups in the population very difficult (in large part for electoral reasons).

Change. How much change is going on? We all like to think that today we live through a period of dramatic social and political upheaval. On objective grounds, our current era seems to have a justifiable claim to this. But consider—and this covers only the West—three periods: 1400–1600, which saw the Hundred Years' War, the Italian Renaissance, the emergence of the modern Westphalian state, and the Reformation and Inquisition; 1770–1850, which witnessed the American and French Revolutions, the Industrial Revolution, and the emergence of modern industrial capitalism; or 1910–50, with two world wars, the rise of Nazism and Communism, ultimately the triumph of social democracy, and the sharpest rise in living standards and life expectancy in the history of the West. Confronted with this, are you still sure you can persuade a historian that we now live in an exceptional age? Our temporal proximity to the contemporary period biases us to see big exceptional changes where they might not be so exceptional after all.

We also face the problem of how to recognize change and its effects. An interesting debate has emerged in political economy over the last few years between proponents of relatively stable different systems of capitalism in the OECD (Hall and Soskice 2001) and those who claim that cosmetic stability hides profound processes of change in substance (Streeck and Thelen 2004). The argument of the first Varieties of Capitalism school is that different capitalist systems may come under pressure and adapt, but that functionally they still operate along lines that reflect the previously existing arrangements. Where everyone asserts change, these authors say, we see remarkable stability. They point out, for example, that the rise of business and the internationalization of finance has done little to undermine Germany's organized form of capitalism. The illusion of change is there because we confuse changes in form with changes in function. (A declaration of interest: I am one of these authors.) The others disagree: something may look like stability, but really is not. Old institutions can be reconfigured; for example, new elements can be introduced that change the way existing elements worked and the way central actors make use of frameworks can lead to outcomes that were not a part of the initial blueprint. Small changes which look insignificant, their general claim is, can have big effects. Everything may look and feel the same, but the interactions between all the constituent elements may make the system as a whole quite different from what it was in the past.

Both these problems—recognizing change and assessing how important it is—alert us to the general issue that any statement that invokes 'change' has to specify a clear metric of change which distinguishes 'large', 'important' from 'small', 'inconsequential' changes. Often, of course, these metrics are contested, as the example above suggests. However, as long as such a metric is reasonable (see Chapter 4 on issues of measurement validity), that is not a problem in itself—but it has to be transparent to other readers so that they can question it if they think it is wrong.

Assume, now, that you have come to the conclusion that something has changed. How do you know that these changes have effects for what you are interested in? Think of the analogy with our body. Because each one of them has a finite lifetime, all the cells in our body change once every several weeks. However, we do not change as a result; in fact, given that such a remarkable and fundamental transformation takes place the whole time, it is quite intriguing that we remain the same. In this case, change is subsumed under functional continuity. But then think of very slow shifts in the composition of the population, often stretching over one or two generations. From one day to the next, not much seems to happen: the shifts are too small to have significant aggregate effects. Let these developments play out over several decades, however, and you end up with a dramatically changed electorate that counts more older than younger people, and where the pension burden on the state and society may reach quite dramatic proportions.

In the social sciences, as this section has suggested, time is not on our side. Everything we study takes place in history, and we have to keep that in mind in our research. Some research designs may allow us to freeze time and thus ignore it, but the problem never entirely disappears. For example, central banks have become very different institutions from what they were in the 1960s, from dependent and expansive back then to the independent and conservative ones we know today. Researchers often ignore such shifts, for example by throwing all these central banks into one data set, at their own peril. Do not do it—or do not do it, at least, without thinking about it first.

Conclusion

This chapter discussed a set of critical issues that we all have to come to terms with when thinking about our research. It started out with the point that there are two very different research traditions in the social sciences: statistical analysis, which sees the world as collections of independent variables and looks for marginal causes and effects; and configurational analysis, which understands the world as consisting of discrete combinations of determining factors. Each of these basic approaches is, in the limiting case, useful for answering different questions, and there are remarkably few bridges between these two methodological traditions. The next section discussed the nature of the universe of cases or data that your research is engaging. Without a good sense of what exists 'out there', and where your empirical material sits in that universe, it is impossible to move beyond the rather anodyne collection of facts for their own sake. But universes do not always come as we want them to. We cannot change history to make our universe larger, and we have to be aware, when we talk about comparability, of how exactly our case(s) speak to each other. History was the theme of the last section: all social science investigates processes that take place in history. We cannot simply suspend time—but the methodological tools we have at our disposal are on the whole quite poor at handling that.

Because of the intrinsic limitations of statistics, exacerbated by the notion that history matters, the tradition of configurational studies, in which we see cases not as collections of independent variables but as discrete combinations of factors, often playing out over time, finds it quite easy to persist in the social sciences. This way of understanding processes is a powerful instrument for dealing with the issue that many factors (may) matter, and that they are likely to matter in particular combinations at particular points in time. Case studies and structured comparisons, the subject of the next chapter, are the tools that social scientists use for that type of analysis. *Qualitative Comparative Analysis*, in turn, is a formalization of these methods, which holds the promise of analysis using the depth of knowledge associated with case studies, relying on the sophistication of rigorous analysis, while respecting the complex, discrete, configurational character of many of the settings that we are interested in. The next chapter lays out the basics of such case studies and structured comparative research.

FURTHER READING TO CHAPTER 2

Ragin's statement (1987: chs. 1–4) of the tension between variable and case-oriented research, and Rueschemeyer et al.'s brilliant exploration (1991) of those issues in studies of economic development and democracy take you a long way towards understanding the basic problems of statistical versus configurational analysis. Braumoeller and Goertz (2000) make explicit the methodology of necessary conditions, and Gary Goertz (2003) writes lucidly about the methodological underpinnings of necessary, sufficient, and INUS conditions. Bill Clark and his colleagues (2006) engage this debate directly from the angle of probabilistic approaches, arguing that statistical analysis can be used as a tool for identifying necessary and sufficient conditions as well. Rohlfing (2008) questions Lieberman's 'nested analysis' (2005) as a good way of dealing with multi-method design, by pointing out some of the pitfalls. Pierson (2004) is *the* book on time in our kind of research, which thinks through questions raised by most sophisticated contemporary scholars who have paid attention to it at some point or other. Streeck and Thelen (2004) on modes of institutional change is a good guide on how different models of change might operate.

3 Constructing Case Studies and Comparisons

Take a random sample of beginning graduate students in political science and ask them how they envision their research. With the exception of a few universities in the world that are famous for their emphasis on quantitative methods, chances are that many of them will say they are thinking of case studies or some form of a two, three, or four case comparison. Ask them why, and the answer is very often that they know at least one of the cases already, have worked on it for their master's degree, and speak the language (the first and the last combined are usually thinly veiled code for 'I come from there'). So the Greek students study Greece, the French study France, the Portuguese Portugal, and very often the United Kingdom or Ireland show up as comparative cases, since—indeed—they speak the language and therefore assume that it cannot be all that hard to acquire the necessary information to make the comparison work. These students find out reasonably quickly that shoehorning the cases into an argument or twisting the theory to make it fit the cases is not all that easy. Speaking the language and having some superficial knowledge of a place may be necessary but certainly not sufficient conditions for doing research on that country or region. Despite the obvious mismatch between the question and the cases at hand, the fixed costs are too high to let go of that particular set-up—the work these researchers have invested in the cases is now working against them—and it often takes more than a year to turn the initial research into something more solid and (sometimes) interesting beyond a small circle of aficionados. That year is the time spent on reconfiguring the cases and rethinking the initial question to such an extent that not much is left of the idea they started out with, but which may provide a good start for a project. In such circumstances, many of them would in fact have done better to stop what they were doing and rethink the project from the bottom up. They have to decide if they want to write a Ph.D. thesis on an interesting problem, and select the cases in light of that, or a thesis on a country and then see what the interesting questions on that country might be? This rather painful process of redesigning the project teaches one crucial lesson: data, cases, and arguments are closely related and ignoring those links leads to problems.

Many Ph.D. projects rely on case studies since, whatever their shortcomings and however much quantitative methods may have colonized large parts of the social sciences, case studies are still pretty much a core part of the stock in trade (Gerring 2001). Case studies offer detailed insights into mechanisms, motives of actors, and constraints they face at particular moments which no other method—statistics, experiment, biographies, or even more systematic comparative analysis—can offer, and they do so for a relatively low price (two to three often funded years of a Ph.D. student's life) compared with large-scale surveys.

There is a problem though: since your sample size is one (or sometimes between, say, one and four, but that does not change the nature of the problem), it is impossible to generalize a theory on the basis of one case (King et al. 1994). The issue is, in simple terms, that you need to be able to know and demonstrate that the case(s) is (are) representative of a wider set of instances in which something similar might happen. The standard way to argue that, usually built on claims that the case is 'typical' of something, thus invoking some soft form of statistical average, too often relies on the 'Believe me, I know' mode of argumentation (but 'believing', I always tell my students, 'is a private matter best done in churches and other temples of worship, not in universities'). Case studies are not made for generalizations, should therefore not be used for that purpose, and intellectual honesty suggests that you simply avoid any reference to that possibility altogether.

Case studies can quite powerfully contribute to building arguments in several other ways. Since case studies are always constructed on the basis of a theory, their selection is therefore explicitly biased and they are *not* randomly chosen. This explicit selection bias means that they can be quite powerful tools to test and/or unpack an existing theory and come up with new, better arguments about causal mechanisms, especially when paired with one or more other cases in the right way. Leaving the idea behind that single cases allow you to generalize opens a door to a much richer, though also more complex, way of using case studies in the social sciences.

This chapter is organized as follows: I will start with a short section on what defines a case and a case study, and then go on to discuss different forms of case studies such as process-tracing and critical case studies. The following section will then lay out the basics of the comparative method as it was canonized by John Stuart Mill, and the chapter finishes with a discussion of *qualitative comparative analysis* (QCA). QCA is best thought of as a method that formalizes Mill's methods of difference and similarity over more than just a handful of cases in which a researcher could know all relevant facts for his or her research. The concluding section wraps up and prepares the ground for the next chapter.

A case of what?

What is a case study? This is not as easy a question to answer as anyone might think (Gerring 2001). Start by thinking of it as the study of a single instance of a decision, policy, institution, event, process, etc.—the study of a single case, in short—in which the case is differentiated from other cases by having a single value (high or low, absent or present, say) in terms of either the outcome that you are interested in or of the explanation that you are exploring. The main reason why this single instance or event is important for you is because it sheds light on a broader theory or argument as a result of how it is connected to that theory or argument. A case can therefore be a person, a country, a region, a city, a company, a sector, a policy, an event—just about anything, as long as it is, as an object of research, limited in time and space, and allows you to say something meaningful beyond the case in question. Methodologically speaking, cases therefore can be defined on the basis of three important characteristics: they are bounded in time and space, the case has to relate to the rest of the world, and case and theory have to be related.

The first chapter discussed how research questions need a clear definition in time and space: they need to have logical and meaningful boundaries. The same is true of cases, and, as a result, the constraints that organized research questions (find logical not chronological beginnings and endings to a research question, do not study the future, choose positive outcomes, etc.) also apply to the way cases are defined. For example, 'Populist politics in Poland since 1989' is, by these criteria, not a well-defined case because the case has an open ending and it is unclear if 'populist politics' also includes standard political parties who adopt 'populist' policies or only 'populist' parties. 'The rise of the *Law and Justice* party (*PiS*) in Poland between 1995 and 2005' is much better: you are explaining the rise to power of the Kaczynski brothers' party from its early days to their electoral victory in 2005, and that might be the particular case that you are looking at to understand the rise of populist politics in Poland after the initial years of the post-1989 transition. You could construct the rise of *PiS* as a culmination of the emergence and evolution of populism in Poland, and the period 1995–2005 could be argued to capture the political dynamics after the immediate post-1989 transition towards a more or less consolidated competitive political system (1995), and the first *PiS* government (2005).

This brings us to the next and perhaps most central point that anyone should ponder when starting a case study, which is: *What is my case a case of*? Recall how I pointed out in the previous chapter that you always have to be able to answer the questions 'what is the relevant universe, and where is the empirical material that I gathered located in that universe?' Let's go back to the example of the *PiS*. Constructing the *PiS* as a case that allows you to understand a wider phenomenon requires that you have a good sense of what that wider phenomenon could be. There are at least two candidates for that, and while they are not necessarily mutually exclusive, they lead to different questions about the relevant universe: the shift towards populism among other Polish parties, or the wider phenomenon of emergent populism in Central European politics. In the case of the first, the *PiS* is regarded as a logical consequence of the slow drift into populism that has characterized the Polish political system, and which has found its way into the traditional parties as much as into newcomers such as the *PiS*. Whether the *PiS* is the leader (pushing the other parties towards populism because of their electoral appeal) or the follower (capitalizing on a populist cleavage that has opened up as a result of the policies of the traditional parties in office) is less important than that the *PiS* heralds the consolidation of the political system sliding into populism. In the case of the second, you will have to figure out what the emergence and triumph of populist policies in Poland (and the *PiS* in particular) might tell you about populist party dynamics elsewhere: what does attention to Poland allow you to say that studying other countries, for example, Slovakia or Hungary, does not allow you to say? At the very least you have to show in this example, *how, where,* and *why* Poland is similar to or different from the others, and where it sits, as it were, in the implicit distribution of cases (in a one-dimensional space, e.g, is it towards the more or the less likely populist political systems?). The third characteristic of the case follows logically from the choice you have just made: once your case is linked to its relevant universe, you can begin to explain how it is linked to a particular theory. Remember that theories have relevant universes (or 'scope conditions', as they are also called), and defining that universe implies choosing a theory that you will engage with your research. Put differently, once you have clearly defined the universe, you have in fact connected empirical observation—the case—to a theory or argument.

Cases and case studies therefore come in many different forms. The first and possibly weakest form of a case—to call it a 'case study' would make too much of this—is one where a case simply illustrates a theory. This is a small but very useful tool to find out if you are on the right track with your working hypothesis: if you cannot come up with a single example that confirms your argument, you probably have a problem. Possibly your argument is correct, but the world just will not produce an outcome that is consistent with it. Too bad: if there is not a single instance, we will never know if your argument is right, even if it is the best thought-out point anyone ever came up with (don't argue 'too bad for the facts'; try another argument). In such an instance of a single example, the case allows you and your argument to pass the simple test of plausibility. The next step up the scale of case studies is one which is slightly more elaborate. After you have established plausibility by finding at least one empirical manifestation of your case, you can explore, without necessarily being conclusive, different empirical manifestations of your argument. You can use case studies as a way of understanding new dimensions to the argument (the outcome, e.g., could be the result of fundamentally different processes than others have said). In such an explorative case study, the onus is on the researcher to bring together in the concluding chapters what he or she sees as the different implications and further specifications, and then lay out clear arguments and hypotheses which can be tested in a new study.

One particularly strong way of using descriptive case studies is a before/after comparison. Imagine you want to find out if non-violent crimes such as car theft, burglaries, robberies, etc. fall once soft drugs are tolerated (i.e. decriminalized). You could compare Amsterdam (or any other large city in the Netherlands) with a similarly sized city in another country, and compare police reports, crime statistics, and criminological studies. But the problem is that these two (or more) cities you'll be comparing do not just differ in that one has a tough policy on drugs while the other a lax one, but also that they are in different countries, with different economies, cultures, histories, etc. Therefore, even if you discovered that crime was lower in Amsterdam than in, say, Marseille, it would be a bit of a push to conclude that it was due to the tolerance of soft drugs. Soft drugs may, to put it mildly, not be the most important social problem in Marseille that could explain crime in the city. Or the Dutch may simply be well-behaved people who do not commit as many crimes as others. So, comparing Amsterdam and other cities leaves a big question mark over your findings. But suppose you found a place where possession of soft drugs was originally considered a criminal offence, but where for a variety of reasons the police has stopped arresting people over possession of small quantities (i.e. where they are tolerated in the same way that they are in the Netherlands). Then you are able to hold everything else constant that made a conclusive comparison between Amsterdam and Marseille so difficult. The local economy, culture, demographics including ethnic composition, social structure, etc., do not change from one day to the next, simply because the police decides to change its attitude towards soft drugs. If you now find that crime rates fell after the introduction of the new policy, you are on much firmer ground to conclude that it was due to the new policy. You can even do more with this set-up: a few years ago possession of soft drugs was effectively decriminalized in one of the London boroughs, but not in other boroughs: the local head of the police did so on the grounds that his police force had plenty of other, far more pressing problems to handle. Now you have great material (the data, not the weed!): not only can you compare the crime rate before and after the policy change in the borough of Lambeth, where drugs were decriminalized, you can also compare the fall in Lambeth with the evolution of crime elsewhere in London. It could have been the case that for some unknown reason crime fell everywhere and then a shift in the drug policy in one borough does not tell you all that much. Or you could check to see if the number and pattern of non-violent crime changed: it is always possible that the Lambeth criminals now operate across the river in Westminster. If you discovered that this was the case, the *prima facie* sensible operation in one part of the city would lead to an increased crime rate elsewhere, and therefore to a mere redistribution rather than reduction of crime, and would require a more subtle way of handling drug-related crimes than simple decriminalization. But whatever you end up with in terms of findings, the before/after comparison has offered you a very powerful and effective way of drawing intelligent conclusions from quite simple descriptive data. (In effect, you set up the relevant comparisons as a 'method of difference' comparative research design—about which more later in this chapter.)

Process-tracing case studies (see Allison [1971] for a classic elaboration) are another way to use studies of single cases as a way of addressing a broader question. They receive their methodological basis in the simple observation that most arguments and theories in (social) science are highly condensed versions of a causal or functional link, along the lines of 'A causes B' (in the sense that if A is present, then B will be present as well and chronologically follow A). But then think of what A and B can be, and you realize that very often it is not immediately clear how they might be related. For example, economic development causes democracy, capitalism causes poverty (or an increase in wealth), etc.—sure, many of us would raise in sceptical tones, but *how* exactly does capitalism cause poverty or wealth, or how does economic development cause democracy? We are in effect asking what the intermediate steps are that constitute the link between such broad and abstract concepts. Go back to an example that I discussed in Chapter 1: 'Does democracy make nations wealthier?' is a pretty straightforward question, which could easily be resolved through statistical analysis. And if you do, you might discover that controlling for everything else, the first-order correlation between democracy and wealth is, say, 0.75 (and for the statistics aficionados, let's say that it is significant at the .01 level, so this is no statistical fluke). No one will deny that this is a seriously strong result—but in this version it is a correlation, almost a functional relationship in fact, not a causal argument. So we need to unpack the argument in a series of connected intermediate steps, which would go more or less like this: since (*step 1*) the median voter in a market economy often has an income below the average, (*step 2*) these voters will vote for parties that favour redistribution from high-income groups in the population to low-income groups, and this, in turn, (*step 3*) leads to higher spending by lower-income groups (the others will save their money), which (*step 4*) results in higher private consumption and therefore aggregate demand, and (*step 5*) therefore higher growth. Each one of these steps can be tested individually, and we can then show, if all of them come out as strong correlations, that democracy leads to higher growth because all of the intermediate steps in the argument have proven to be strong correlations. Note, though, that you have established correlations within a strong argument, but not really a causal argument.

Process-tracing case studies adopt a similar logic, but pay more attention to the causal detail: we start with the most parsimonious, almost minimalist, version of a causal argument, and then try to understand the deeper mechanisms that a theory purports to explain or understand by analysing the causality for each of these steps. Theories are often implicit about what the exact mechanisms are; process-tracing allows us to state those explicitly and qualify them where necessary. Such case studies will go down the causal chain, reconstructing the steps in the chain, and then demonstrating, for example, how, at particular critical junctures, the decisions or choices that were made confirmed or disconfirmed the basic mechanisms that the argument is exploring. Graham Allison's case study (1971) on the Cuban missile crisis in 1961 did exactly that. It tried to test three theories on government decision-making in times of international crisis. The first treated governments as rational actors who weigh all the options before engaging in an action or response, the second said that governments have limited information but bureaucratically defined lines of action that are mobilized to rationalize the actions, and the third that responses to such international crises reflect internal politicking inside the government. By examining material that covered the different steps in the decision-making process of both the US and the USSR governments and evaluating the three theories in that light, Allison concluded that the latter of the three options gave us the better tools to understand how the crisis emerged and developed.

Process-tracing therefore involves not just detailed examination of the material, but also weighing the evidence in light of the different theories. That means not just looking at the material but also making explicit what type of material is suggested by different theories and searching for that evidence. Once you have then concluded which one of the theories works best by confronting the available data with the different arguments, you can then use that insight as a way to generalize to other cases. When that works, the single case has produced an explanation that ought to be helpful in understanding many other, similarly structured, situations. Your more general theory is then that governments who are faced with a crisis do not necessarily weigh all the options rationally and then decide (the idea at the basis of mutual deterrence) but often make decisions that reflect internal divisions between senior politicians on how to deal with such crises.

Critical case studies: challenging a theory

Of all the research designs that rely on single case studies, the critical case study (alternatively also known as a 'crucial' or 'limiting' case) is a very powerful one (Eckstein 1975). Its logical structure is remarkably simple, but it can go a long way. Two ingredients are needed. The first one is a theory or argument at a high level of specification, which says that under a set of reasonably well-defined conditions, A causes B (or B occurs). The second element is a case which conforms in every relevant instance to these conditions that the theory has specified, but where the outcome is different from the one that the theory predicted. By picking a case that conforms to the theory in every relevant dimension, you have started by stacking the cards *against you* and in favour of the argument you are up against. If you then demonstrate that even under these 'most likely' circumstances for the causality or argument to hold it does not, the theory must have deeply problematic sides. Think through carefully what the logical structure of such a design is: you selected your case explicitly on the basis of theory, not on a random basis. The theory you are up against in fact gave you the relevant universe of cases, which were all drawn from among those where the theory or argument should, as far as we know, be valid. But you found a case where the causality did not hold, and as far as we can tell, there was no reason why the case should not conform to the causality or the theory that you were trying to test. Put differently, the case is well within the universe as defined by the theory, and your finding therefore throws into question the theory as a whole. It may not be entirely wrong, and it usually is not, since it managed to make sense of a large part of the world; however, your material and the interpretation you give helps you specify better how exactly the old theory worked, under which conditions it holds and when not, and how your new view incorporates the aberrant puzzling case that you introduced. (The structure of the design is comparable but inverted in a 'least likely' setting: you find a case where A causes B in conditions where the theory suggested that this was not supposed to happen.)

We have already come across versions of this research design earlier: think back to Max Weber's research on the spirit of capitalism: by studying the United States, which Marxists saw as the most important global capitalist nation, Weber implicitly also attacked the causal mechanisms, such as class struggle, that were central to the Marxist interpretation of the emergence of capitalism. If, the argument goes, even in the United States religion played a crucial role in the establishment of capitalism, it was likely to have been important in places where old religious traditions were stronger and rational individualism weaker. Critical case research designs have a long pedigree, as Weber's example suggests, and some of the classics in the social sciences have drawn on it to good effect. In his classic study *Political Parties*, for example, in which Robert Michels (1915) developed the *Iron Law of Oligarchy*, he relied on the unquestionable pro-democracy credentials of social-democratic parties as a window into the organizational dynamics of all parties. If you reasonably assume that social-democratic parties are in favour of an extension of political and economic democracy, you would expect them to have especially democratic internal procedures. (Note that this is not necessarily true of other parties on the left: Communists at the time believed in the vanguard role of the party, which requires discipline and centralized command.) Michels then discovered that this was not the case: leaders dominated the social-democratic parties in exactly the same way as happened in more conservative parties, in large measure as a result of the professionalization of the party. Thus his Iron Law: 'who says organisation, says oligarchy'.

There are two implications worth exploring a little more in depth. Critical case studies fully exploit the adversarial way of making your argument: they force you to think through carefully what the strongest version of the opposite argument to yours might be, build that into the way you engage empirical material, and then show it is problematic. Instead of simply finding corroborative evidence for your point, you show how and why another argument is wrong and why your argument, which can make sense of the aberration while the prevailing view cannot, is better. By stacking the cards against you, that is, by thinking through what the best possible alternative to your argument would be, and then coming out on top, you have done a lot more than simply showing that your way of looking at the world is logically better or squares with the facts.

The second is that critical case designs are asymmetric. If a critical case design is conclusive at all (a view that is not entirely unchallenged, see King et al. [1994]), its main logical function is to disprove or refute a theory: it states that even under very likely conditions, the theory does not hold. (Note that the alternative, demonstrating that even under very unlikely conditions a theory still holds, is a valuable contribution but not as strong a point, since we already knew that the theory was valid.) Refuting a theory is, however, only half the work. Assuming you convincingly demonstrate that an argument does not hold under such likely conditions, you still have to think through what you are adding to the theory. You have to find a dimension that was incorrectly specified in the old theory, and which helps you understand what actually happened— why, in other words, your case ended up on the wrong side of the argument. That re-specification of the theory is as crucial as the first step. It is the argument you contribute; in a Lakatosian universe, it is your T2, which captures most of the variation under T1, but accommodates the aberrant fact F.

Consider the following example: Wolfgang Streeck (1996) tried to find out if and how convergence in terms of organizational and work practices might occur in the car industry. The car industry offers a critical case: it is a mature industry, competing internationally, and there seems to be an organizational model that is accepted as 'best practice', that is, which leads to the most efficient outcomes. In such a case, according to the theory, convergence in the organization of workplaces is very likely to occur, since small differences in efficiency can lead to gains and losses in market share and all producers want to increase market share and avoid the latter. Streeck then analysed in detail how the German and Japanese car industries operate and adjusted to international competition. His basic observation—the refutation of convergence theory—is that the same pressures in different institutional settings have led to different outcomes, and that

Japanese and German car factories are still very different, despite the fact that the Japanese seem to have a competitive advantage. His counter-argument, which makes sense of the puzzling observation, is that those processes of industrial change are socially and institutionally embedded, and thus reflect the nature of the political–economic system that they are a part of.

Critical case studies are not walking down the street, ready to be picked up. Like every other strategy with regard to research design, they are constructions by the researcher, in this particular instance possibly *par excellence*. The particular formulation of the theory and the organization of the data are both your work: the theory has to be translated into a set of relevant conditions under which a particular causality holds, while the empirical material should be reorganized in such a way that it speaks directly to that formulation of the theory. Critical cases have to be con-structed, in other words—or better: empirical material has to be presented in such a way that it speaks to a theory in this particular way.

Critical case designs are, as a result of their potential power, very useful research strategies for a graduate research project. They are economical but with potentially big effects, since they strongly question a theory, on the basis of one case, while leaving open exploration of other arguments. They also allow a researcher to start developing early on the necessary 'two legs' that matter in a further career: the substantive area of the case (the country, the policy, the sector, etc.) and the theoretical issues in the (sub-) discipline that the case engages. Imagine, for example, that you find a vibrant democratic system in a very poor country which has a history of ethnic strife. If all goes well, your Ph.D. research will contribute to theories of how democracy comes about by exploring a set of conditions under which poor, ethnically divided countries have been able to democratize (whilst the prevailing theories suggested that to be close to impossible), and you learn a lot about that country and possibly about the continent where the country is located.

But critical cases can be hard work, since you need to show very carefully that the case material actually engages the theory in the way that you claim, without turning the theory into a silly straw man that can be blown over with one puff of wind. Furthermore, beginning researchers usually already have invested quite a bit in their topic and potential cases, without thinking through carefully how that material would engage theories in a three-cornered fight. The problem then shifts from constructing a critical case design out of the blue to reorganizing the material that you already have so that it begins to approximate it. In such a situation it may happen that you discover that the single case does not allow itself to be recast as a critical case: the articulation of your material and the theory you are up against just does not work like that. Don't despair yet: that suggests that you need to rethink your research design by bringing in more cases. From implicit comparisons with the cases covered by the theory you are arguing against, you have to start thinking about how to design explicit comparisons.

Comparative research: Mill's methods of difference and of agreement

What is comparative research? Let us start, somewhat counter-intuitively, by saying what it is not. Very often research involving two or more cases is treated as if it is comparative research. In many cases, however, these are not much more than multiple case studies, conducted independently of one another, with a conclusion which engages the two cases side by side, and then says what your findings in one case help understand about the other, where they agree and where they disagree. Comparative research is something different and more ambitious: in a parallel way to how case selection allows you to increase analytical leverage, comparative research requires an active intervention by the researcher to select the cases in such a way that they allow for a conclusive answer of the question you are asking.

One useful way you can do that is by stating the cases as a paradox, or at the very least as having a counter-intuitive outcome. Two countries, say, were at a similar starting point in 1970, but ended up being very different by 2000; explaining this somewhat unexpected difference is a good start. Or better still, you argue that a well-established theory would predict that case A ends up in position X and case B in position Y; but the opposite happened. Explaining this paradoxical outcome is a good way of setting up a comparative research design. The main reason why such comparative designs work well is that they rely on two or more cases, and you compare them with each other to shed light on a theory that everyone more or less took for granted.

Let us formalize this insight a little by making comparisons across different dimensions more explicit. The basic idea behind such an approach is given by what John Stuart Mill, in *A System of Logic*, called the methods of difference and of agreement (see also Skocpol [1984: 378 ff.]). Note, however, that in the form in which they appear below, they are subject to a few important assumptions. One is that the possible explanations are independent of one another, that is, they will have individual effects and no joint effects. Cases of *complex causation*, where effects emerge as a result of combinations of possible explanatory factors, are impossible to determine with this set-up. The second is that outcomes are always the result of the same causes; cases of *equifinality*, where the same outcome can be reached by different (combinations of) factors are equally hard to examine with these methods. QCA, the subject of the next question, as well as statistics may be ways to handle those problems.

Method of difference. In the method of difference you select two cases that are similar in every relevant characteristic except for two, the first being the outcome that you are trying to explain (the 'dependent variable' or DV in Tables 3.1–3.3) and the second what you think explains this outcome (the 'independent variable' or IV). The logic is that, since you hold everything else constant, other possible explanations cannot explain the variation in the outcome: only the variation (difference) in the explanation that you propose can explain the variation in the outcome. Table 3.1 presents this logical structure schematically.

Take the following example to illustrate this logic. Suppose you want to assess the impact of proportional representation (PR) on party systems and government formation. The idea underlying this is quite simply that a majoritarian system usually leads to a two-party system (only winners receive seats) and that government formation in such an instance is simply a matter of finding out who won the majority in parliament, whereas a PR system produces a parliament with more than two parties, which usually implies coalitions and therefore more complicated government platforms and a longer time for governments to be formed. One way to go about this is to find two countries which can be constructed as being very similar in all relevant dimensions. They are roughly the same size, for example, with a similar demography and economy, and have the same

Table 3.1 Method of difference

	Case A	Case B
Explanation 1	Present	Present
Explanation 2	High	High
Explanation 3	Present	Present
Explanation 4	Low	Low
Explanation 5	Absent	Absent
Explanation N ('IV')	**Absent** (low)	**Present** (high)
Outcome ('DV')	*Absent*	*Present*

spectrum of political parties (in Table 3.1 this would refer to 'Explanation 1' through 'Explanation 5'). However, one has a majoritarian first-past-the-post electoral system, and the other a PR system ('Explanation N' in Table 3.1). You then find out if there are systematic differences in party strength and government composition or government formation: which parties are strong and weak?; is government formation faster or slower in one or the other?; are the same parties in government?, etc. Since you isolated all the other possible relevant explanations (which is exactly what you do if you make sure they are the same across these two cases), the differences between the two countries in terms of party system and government must be due to the different electoral systems.

In practical terms, you often construct the method of difference design the other way around. Rather than looking for two cases which are the same on every relevant dimension except for the one that you want to emphasize, you have discovered an unexpected difference in outcome between two cases, and you then try to find out how similar these cases are, paying special attention to those dimensions that others have alerted us to in the past (i.e. the function of the literature review in such a project). If all goes well, and you can show that the two are very similar on those *a priori* relevant dimensions, you have constructed a method of difference research design by increasing 'comparability': you have reconstructed the cases in such a way that a comparison between them becomes meaningful and allows you to draw firm conclusions.

Method of Agreement. The method of agreement works the other way around: everything between the two cases is different, except for the explanation and the outcome. Since all other potentially relevant dimensions vary, but your outcomes are the same, only the similarities between cases on the explanation can cause the agreement between the cases in terms of outcomes. An example might again be helpful. Suppose that you want to find out if labour market reforms have played a role in reducing unemployment. You start out by locating two countries which are very different in terms of possible explanations that others have come up with. One is a large economy and the other is a small one, one is highly open and the other relatively closed, female labour market participation varies between high and low, one has an independent central bank and the other a dependent one, one a Left and the other a Right government, etc. If both have made their labour markets more flexible, and if unemployment is low in both, you can be quite confident that labour market reforms played a role in determining the unemployment rate. It could be—as I happen to think—that the argument is wrong, but that is not your problem: someone else will point it out, and design a study that brings in a new dimension that was not part of the argument up until then. But up to that point, you have made your contribution. Table 3.2 presents the basic logic of the Method of Agreement.

Most of the time, however, cases do not present themselves in such a neat way: they are almost never entirely the same or different except for two dimensions. That is not a disaster: what you can do in such a situation is include another case in your research design which allows you to make smaller, more focused bilateral comparisons on relevant dimensions. By introducing such a shadow case, you filter out, step by step as it were, the effect of singular variables. A *shadow case* offers you the variation that you are interested in only on the dimension(s) that were unclear from the initial crisp comparison between the two cases. In other words, it does not entail a full-fledged case study, but helps you explore—'in the shadow' of

Table 3.2 Method of agreement

	Case A	Case B
Explanation 1	Absent	Present
Explanation 2	Low	High
Explanation 3	Present	Absent
Explanation 4	High	Low
Explanation 5	Present	Absent
Explanation N ('IV')	**Present** (high)	**Present** (high)
Outcome ('DV')	*Present*	*Present*

the other cases—what was not entirely conclusive from the initial design. You may wonder why you do not need to go back to the complete version of the comparison but can sort out this problem with partial comparisons between your initial cases and a shadow case. Use Table 3.3 as a guide to follow the argument. First off, we already know that Explanations 1 through 4 cannot explain the variation we see in the outcome, since between cases A and B they do not vary, while the outcomes in the two cases do (hence they show up in brackets in Table 3.3). We can therefore treat those as unimportant—put differently, all we are interested in is the variation across *Explanation 5, Explanation N,* and the *Outcome.* Now look at those three possible explanations across the three cases. What we see is that in case C, the configuration on these three dimensions combines the constellations found in cases A and B, but in an interesting way which contains much of the information that we need. Case C suggests that Explanation 5 cannot explain the outcome for two reasons. One is that vis-à-vis case A the variation is the wrong way around: Explanation 5 is 'absent' in both A and C, but the outcome varies across these two cases; furthermore, a comparison between cases B and C indicates that the variation between these two on Explanation 5 cannot explain the same outcome (which is 'present' in both B and C). Since the shadow case has quite conclusively shown that Explanation 5 cannot explain the outcome that you found, and since we already knew that Explanations 1 through 4 cannot either, only Explanation N can do that.

Consider the example of the different effects of electoral systems discussed earlier. Two countries are roughly the same size, with a similar demography and economy, and have a similar spectrum of political parties, *but* they differ not only in that one has a majoritarian first-past-the-post electoral system, and the other a PR system, but also in that one has a highly fractious ethnic composition while the other is ethnically quite homogenous. Knowing that the possible explanations on which the cases do not vary cannot explain any variation in terms of government formation that we may find, we can now concentrate on the role that ethnic divisions may play. Suppose we find a case which is ethnically divided and has a PR system, and government formation takes just as long and follows the same pattern as the PR country which was ethnically homogenous. That suggests quite strongly that ethnic divisions do not matter, but that the electoral system does.

Table 3.3 Method of difference, multiple determinants, and shadow case

	Case A	Case B	Case C
Explanation 1	Present	Present	(Present)
Explanation 2	High	High	(Low)
Explanation 3	Present	Present	(Absent)
Explanation 4	Low	Low	(Low)
Explanation 5	*Absent*	*Present*	*Absent*
Explanation N ('IV')	**Absent** (low)	**Present** (high)	**Present** (high)
Outcome ('DV')	*Absent*	*Present*	*Present*

In principle, nothing stops you from continuing this exercise for each of the relevant dimensions where the comparison is inconclusive. But the problem is that the more such possible alternative explanations are introduced as shadow cases, the messier the whole research design becomes (and the harder your work is, since you need strong qualitative material to make the point, which often means that you need to spend time in libraries, archives, do interviews, etc.). In fact, when the number of cases increases as much as this, you gradually move from comparisons of (very) small numbers of cases to medium-number comparisons (between, say, 5 and 30). Such a situation—more than two or three cases but less than what is necessary for a sophisticated statistical analysis—is at the basis of a method and technique called *Qualitative Comparative Analysis* (QCA): this technique treats cases as consistent configurations of dimensions rather than as collections of independent variables and then sees how combinations of these dimensions add to the outcome.

Qualitative comparative analysis: studying cases as configurations

'Quantitative' social scientists—at least those who are positively predisposed—often see 'qualitative' social scientists as those who may well know a lot, but do not always know very well what to do with what they know, since there are no standards that they can use to systematize their material and then generalize from it. Assume for a moment that there is agreement across these two groups that in some instances of research, statistical analysis is not going to get you anywhere because the question or the data just do not allow that; the 'quants' then quite rightly ask the others how they can know that what they find is not purely random, or worse, an arbitrary outcome of the researcher having stacked everything in his or her favour? Case studies and small-N comparative analysis can produce interesting and sometimes even conclusive answers, as the previous sections of this chapter argued. But a lot of these research designs may be limiting, either because they are restricted to the analysis of one or two cases, or because there remains the nagging doubt that other factors beside those identified might matter. Extending cases and possible explanations is the only way to go then. QCA is the research design, strategy, and technique to help you with that (Ragin 1987). Let us start by comparing the following two statements—think through how they differ:

(a) 'When a dictator dies, and there is more than one successor, and the army brass is divided, there is a 95 per cent chance that the country will embark on a transition to democracy.'

(b) 'Botogonia became a democracy in 1997 because dictator Richardson died, his two sons argued over the succession, and the top generals in the army started quarrelling; that gave the opposition a chance to organize a peaceful coup, and write a constitution which allowed them to call elections in early 1998.'

At first glance, both statements seem to be saying the same thing; statement (a) appears to be more general since it seems to talk about places outside Botogonia as well, while expression (b) appears a little more certain, since it explains quite precisely what happened in Botogonia in 1997 and 1998. On the whole, however, the substance of both statements appears very similar in terms of the conditions they identify for the collapse of a dictatorial regime and a transition to democracy. But look again: there is an important difference between the two which we have already come across earlier in Chapter 2: the first one is a probabilistic statement, which lays out the likelihood of something occurring given several factors and their combinations, while the second one says that the outcome (transition to democracy in Botogonia) is explained by a combination of three conditions (death of a dictator, fight between two heirs, quarrel among top army brass), and suggests that all three conditions have to be present for the dictatorial regime in Botogonia to collapse. Put differently, the author of statement (a) could have written (a*) 'When a dictator dies and there is more than one successor, there is a 55 per cent chance that the country will embark on a transition to democracy', and we would have considered that a perfectly reasonable statement. It corrected for the effect that divisions within the army, which did not exist, but which we know from statement (a) to be potentially important, may have had for the outcome. But it is hard to imagine us taking very seriously (b*) 'Botogonia *almost* became a democracy in 1997 when dictator Richardson died, and his two sons argued over the succession, but the top generals in the army remained united; that *almost* gave the opposition a chance to organize a peaceful coup, *almost* write a constitution which allowed them *almost* to call elections in early 1998'. This does not mean that (b*) is wrong. In fact, it may well be a perfect description of the world; the problem is that it simply does not improve our understanding of conditions for successful democratic transitions by a lot. A strategy that makes perfect sense between statements (a) and (a*), which consists in adjusting the probabilities if explanatory factors are added or subtracted, sounds quite strange when translated from (b) to (b*). A statement like (b) was just not made for the world we are interested in. (This example is adapted from Ragin [1987]; I will go back to Ragin's original in a moment.)

Now imagine that there are three other countries in the world where a successful transition takes place. Botogonia's neighbour Matagonia also moves to a democracy when its dictator dies, the three sons have a succession fight, and the top army brass is divided over socio-economic policy. And that something similar happens in Afrizinia and in Tiberia. Lots of things may well be different across these four hypothetical cases: for example, they may be on different continents, two of them may have had support from the United States, one of them is a relatively wealthy country while the other three are poor, and two were democracies before while the other two had never experienced democratic rule. In all four, however, a combination of a dictator's death, quarrels among heirs, and a division within the top brass of the army were present, and in all four democracy ensued. If these four are the cases in your sample, you can draw a probabilistic conclusion along the lines of (a) above—but the more precise statement would be (c) 'A country makes the transition from dictatorship to democracy when the dictator dies, there is a succession fight among heirs, and the top army brass is divided' (assume, for the sake of convenience, that there is a viable opposition in each of these countries). The reason why this is a more accurate statement is that you have identified a set of *necessary conditions* for the transition from dictatorship to democracy which holds in all cases you know of where a transition to democracy took place.

This way of thinking about the world is at the basis of QCA. QCA is a research design, method and strategy which is especially well-suited to small to medium-N universes where explanations are likely to be complex, multidimensional, and configurational, but where statistical analysis is impossible because of straightforward data limitations such as too few cases, or indirect ones such as more possible explanations than available cases. What follows concentrates on the simplest form, known in the trade as 'crisp-set QCA' (as opposed to 'fuzzy-set QCA') (read the excellent book by Ragin [1987] for a more detailed introduction; Schneider and Wagemann [2007] for more on QCA). In its simplest form, QCA divides our complex world into a set of relevant dimensions of cases, and then dichotomizes scores across cases on the basis of the presence or absence (or high/low value) of a relevant dimension. These combinations are then treated as logical possibilities and the cases are, as it were, reconstructed on the basis of the profile they have in this reconstructed universe. They are not 'chopped up' into little pieces as statistics would do, but retain their integrity as a case. To 'score' cases, you ask such questions as 'is X present or absent?'; 'does the country score high or low on Y'; etc., and then build a table that summarizes these scores for your cases—such a table is called a 'truth table' in QCA. Table 3.4 is an example of a truth table borrowed from Ragin (1987: 90).

Table 3.4. is packed with information and might seem hard to digest at first, but a few seconds of analysis leads to a simple, straightforward, and incontrovertible conclusion: if a dictator dies, if there is a conflict between younger and older officers in the military, if the CIA does not like the regime anymore, or if any of these three conditions occur in combinations of two or three, the regime collapses and democracy follows. Why? Because any combination of columns A, B, or C which includes at least one '1' in the truth table, also leads to a '1' in the 'Regime failure' column F, while the absence of all three leaves things unchanged (i.e. leads to a 0 in column F).

Let us complicate things a little by looking at another example of a truth table (Table 3.5), also borrowed from Ragin (1987: 96), which deals with

Table 3.4 Hypothetical truth table showing three causes of regime failure

Condition			Regime failure	Number of instances
A	B	C	F	
0	0	0	0	9
1	0	0	1	2
0	1	0	1	3
0	0	1	1	1
1	1	0	1	2
1	0	1	1	1
0	1	1	1	1
1	1	1	1	3

Note: 0 = absent; 1 = present.
A = Conflict between older and younger military officers
B = Death of a powerful dictator
C = CIA dissatisfaction with the regime
Source: From Ragin (1987: 90).

the determinants of successful strikes. Analysing rows 2 and 3 (marked with * in the table) suggests one of the most counter-intuitive findings in the table: you would expect a large strike fund to lead to a successful strike (the score for strike in column F is 1, again marked with *); however, you discover that there have been successful strikes without a large strike fund. In addition, checking rows 6 and 7 (marked with °), you find that a large strike fund did not necessarily produce a successful strike (the score for strike in column F is 0 for both cases; this is marked with °). The size of the strike fund appears to be relative—in the sense that it may look large, but not if an employer can sit out even a very long strike because he or she has, for example, more than a year's stocks of products in the warehouses and the market for the product is not doing all that well. To such an employer a strike might, in the short run, even be beneficial because it allows him or her to run down stocks without having to pay wages. Conversely, if the product market is booming (rows 1, 3, and 4, marked with †), the employer cannot hold out very long without losing market share, and then the size of a strike fund does not seem to matter all that much (the score for 'successful strike' in these cases in column F is 1). The impact of a strike fund is, in other words, conditional upon the situation that the company is in: when the company is doing well, it does not harm, but a large strike fund is not a guarantee for a successful strike.

Table 3.5 Hypothetical truth table showing three causes of successful strikes

Condition			Successful strike	Number of instances
A	B	C	F	
1†	0	1	1	6
0	1	0*	1*	5
1†	1	0*	1*	2
1†	1	1	1	3
1	0	0	0	9
0	0	1°	0°	6
0	1	1°	0°	3
0	0	0	0	4

Note: 0 = absent; 1 = present.
A = Booming product market
B = Threat of sympathy strikes
C = Large strike fund
Source: From Ragin (1987: 96).

You could, in principle, describe for each of the factors above how they have to be combined with others to have positive or negative effects for the striking workers, and write down those combinations as Boolean equations. After some basic Boolean arithmetic (the details of that are given in the book written by Ragin [1987]) you can show which combinations lead to, in this case, successful strikes, and which ones do not. What remains to do from now on is nothing more than tallying up the combinations, select those which make sense, and you have a fairly good idea of the determinants of successful strikes. Those, then, can be written up in a parsimoniously minimized form, and that is your (set of) argument(s).

These examples suggest that QCA is not just a technique for analysing small and medium-N data (although it could be used just for that if need be), but also forces you to look at the world with different eyes. You are thinking about the world in terms of conditions and discrete sets of conditions which produce relatively clear-cut discrete (absent/present or 0/1) outcomes. Since a lot of the social and political world is organized in that way, that is, in relatively few cases with relatively stable constitutional and institutional arrangements, and produces outcomes which could be understood as present/absent or high/low, QCA is potentially a very powerful research strategy and analytical technique. But it is not an easy one; Boolean algebra is relatively simple, at least in terms of what you would need it for here, but you need to think it through as a logical problem, not simple equations, and most importantly, getting to the point where you can put a '1' or a '0' for a particular case in a truth table may take a lot of reading, interview, and archival work to reconstruct how the case has evolved.

In my honest opinion, QCA should be awarded a Grammy for best 'new kid on the block'. It resolves several pernicious problems in the social sciences in one go, and does so in a way that makes it at least as sophisticated and systematic as statistical analysis could be at its best (though on very different epistemological grounds). Moreover, recent developments among the QCA community suggest that mathematical sophistication is growing fast. The only thing missing is for that promise to materialize: there are, as of yet, very few substantive breakthroughs associated with QCA. So, yes, hold your breath; but do understand that the social sciences are, well, political as well as analysis: the conservatism associated with statistical analysis in political science makes it unlikely that it will receive the Grammy anytime soon—but I am willing to put money on it.

Conclusion

This chapter has dealt with the small-N and medium-N world in social science research, and discussed some of the basics of case-based research, different types of case studies and what they can offer, different comparative designs, and QCA. I showed—here—that case studies can be just as rigorous as statistical analysis, but that this means that researchers have to intervene actively in the way they set up the cases and comparisons. They have to construct their cases in a persuasive way, following basic rules of transparency, and within the broader Lakatosian framework that has been at the basis of this book. Under those circumstances, any broad-minded social scientist will take the material gathered and presented seriously, and engage in a substantive argument on the findings you present. In fact, sometimes—and possibly considerably more often than we care to admit—case studies and research designs based on case studies may be vastly superior to quantitative techniques, because of the way the world presents itself. Methodological rigour is not distinctive of statistical analysis—it is thinking about your research while you're doing it.

Constructing cases and a research design requires more than just some brilliant insights, of course. You need to know quite well what cases look like when thinking about your argument and your research design. Despite what you may have learnt about theory begetting hypotheses, which beget operationalizations, which then lead to measurement (it is hard to believe that research is still taught in this way today, but unfortunately too often it still is), data are a crucial part of thinking through which question you want to ask and how you want to answer it. All methods I know of in the social sciences, and especially in configurational designs, require you to think through cases and arguments in light of some form of data. A sense of data is, in other words, a prerequisite for constructing a persuasive research design and convincing arguments. That is the central problem of the next chapter.

FURTHER READING TO CHAPTER 3

John Gerring has, quite rightly, carved out a reputation of intelligent thinking about case studies. Gerring [2001] and Gerring 2007 are, in my opinion, among the best pieces in that regard. Hall (2004) links the discussions about sophisticated falsificationism to process-tracing in case studies. Eckstein (1975) is the locus classicus for the critical case study. Read also the sceptical comments by King et al. (1994) on critical cases for a counterpoint. John Stuart Mill's *A System of Logic* offers the first statement of the methods of difference and agreement. Skocpol (1984) is the contemporary version that rehabilitated this. In Skocpol (1979), she also explains the logic of shadow cases and uses them more or less in the way I suggest in Chapter 3.

Charles Ragin (1987, 2000, and 2008) is the father of QCA and these texts are foundational. There is a vibrant virtual community of QCA aficionados: check www. compasss.org. Schneider and Wagemann (2007) is a solid textbook on QCA that can help everyone on their way.

4 **Constructing Data**

'When I was interviewing the head of the nationalist party, Mr Smith, he told me that I was right: his political party did X because of Y, just as I had predicted, so I wrote it in my dissertation. During the defence, however, one of the readers asked me if there was any corroborating evidence to that statement which was available to the readers of the thesis, and I told him I did not need that, since the guy who was in charge of the political party had actually told me what they had done and why. They sent me off with the message to use the next year to think about how to make that claim stick. What more did these guys want from me? I got it from the horse's mouth!' The thesis jury in this imaginary chat in the pub may have looked unfair to John, but they had a more than reasonable point: Smith may or may not have told the truth—and there is no *a priori* reason to assume he had not—but that was not good enough for them. They were asking John to show them that what he discovered during that interview was good enough to hang a whole thesis on, since in the way John had presented his material, it failed to meet the basic criteria that would allow them to conclude that. Fortunately, what happened to John is rare—though far from non-existent. We all have an intuition about what went wrong in John's thesis defence, and by making explicit what went wrong, this chapter offers a tool kit to help you avoid making those mistakes in your own work.

At this point, you should have an idea about how to build a viable research question, how to select the cases you are looking for in light of the question you ask, a sense of the availability of data, and of the way you engage the debate. You also have, as a result of your pre-research, a reasonably good idea of what you think is going on. More or less hard data are what you need now. How, then, do you obtain good primary and secondary material? With that innocuous question, a whole new set of problems emerges. Data are not walking down the street, waiting to be picked up (if they were, as in the joke of the two economists who spot a $10 bill on the pavement, no one would believe it, since they would have been snatched up by someone else a long time ago). At best, data have to be found; usually, however, they have to be constructed, more often than not from a very thin basis.

Many beginning Ph.D. students treat this issue slightly more casually than they should. The standard answer to probing how they will find out about what they are doing research on, is often a variation on the statement that shows up in research proposals as 'The method applied here will rely on interviews and archives'. Such answers are, in the words of Agatha Christie's sleuth Hercule Poirot, 'most unsatisfactory'. As we saw in the first chapter, constructing a good research question is near impossible without some sense of data, and the previous two chapters argued that case selection relies on a good sense of the relevant universe—another process which requires data of some form. Finally, even statistical data that allow you to develop a close relationship with your office chair and computer during your thesis work usually have to be understood before they can be used and are almost never ready for immediate consumption. Thinking about data is, in other words, not so much the next stage in research design as an integral part of your research question and what followed from that.

This chapter deals with data, understood here as any form of systematic empirical observation that will help you answer your question. It starts out with the basic methodological issues at the most general level, which are the same regardless of whether your research is based on statistical or configurational analysis (much of that section chimes with what you can find in King et al. [1994: 23–8]). Since arguments need to be thought of in terms of observable implications, the link between concept and data is crucial. That is the problem of validity. Data also have to be reliable: others should see the same things as you did if they were looking for them in the same way that you did. And they need to be replicable: in principle, others should have access to the data and conclude similar things from them that you did. This basic discussion is followed by three sections with a more practical approach that describe how the notions of validity, reliability, and replicability manifest themselves in existing data-sets and in sources with more noise such as interviews.

The key problems: validity, reliability, and replicability

The key problem with John's statement above is that he went, to put things mildly, rather quickly and uncritically from a theory (Y caused X, 'just as I had predicted') to the conclusion that, since Smith told him that such was indeed the case, his hypothesis was right. As far as we know, John never thought about the possibility of asking Smith if, perhaps, factor Z was important as well in why they did X. If John had done his homework, he would have tried to find out from Smith why, then, Z did not matter, knowing that it had done so for a similar political party in another country, or for another party in the same country. Taking statements on faith, perhaps accompanied by a slight raise of the eyebrow, may be helpful when we have a discussion in the pub or at the Christmas lunch/dinner table, but in the job we do, we do not take statements on trust (many scenes in Woody Allen movies that involve unhappy couples on the brink of a divorce may help you think through what would happen if we consistently questioned the veracity of the people that are dear to us). But we are hard on ourselves and others when it comes to research findings. We want to make sure that they actually cover the way we have been thinking about a problem, that what people tell us is more or less true as far as we can tell, and that others would see it like that too if they were looking at it from the vantage point where we stand.

Validity, the first criterion of these three, refers to whether the concepts as you defined them are correctly expressed in the measurements you use. Sometimes this is rather simple: the daily calorie intake is a good indicator of the quality of a diet, and that is, in turn, a pretty good indicator of the general standard of living; so differences between countries or over time in the calories consumed by individuals give you a good indication of variations over time or space in the standard of living of entire populations. Similarly, real GDP growth is a good indicator of the general state of the economy, and definitely much better than any derived or partial indicator such as the net number of new companies or the unemployment rate. (You rely on real and not nominal GDP growth for this, since you want to correct for the way prices move up or down.)

Some concepts, however, are harder to translate into comparable data. Take *affluence*, for example. Perhaps the simplest way to measure this would be to combine some indicator of average income with an indicator of income (in)equality: this would tell you how rich the country is, and how wealth is distributed across the population, thus making it a reasonably valid way to measure affluence in and across countries such as the OECD which have a similar level of economic development. But in sub-Saharan Africa, that measure is not going to get you very far, for the simple reasons that you cannot trust basic statistics in many of the countries in that region, and that much economic activity is not expressed in monetary terms but in kind (a wealthy head of a tribe would measure his or her wealth in terms such as the number of livestock).

Since many middle-income countries often have a large informal economy, it may be that for those as well, the idea of using GDP per capita and income distribution as an indicator of the spread of affluence may be deeply misleading. In an intriguing review of these issues, Fred Block (1990) concluded that even post-industrial societies of the OECD type no longer do all that well in measuring basic economic processes. If a lot of work does not take place in the salaried sector but in voluntary associations, standard measures of GDP will systematically understate certain activities as opposed to others. In a similar vein, feminist welfare state scholars have consistently pointed out that GDP indicators should be revised to include unpaid work by women in an economy, usually within the family.

There are organizations that have as one of their main tasks to produce synthetic indicators of such complex, often multidimensional concepts: economic freedom (Fraser Institute), for example, democracy (Freedom House), or competitiveness (Davos). While many of these are useful as a first crack at the issue, always remember—I will discuss this in considerably more detail in the next section—that these indicators were not designed for your but for their goals, and that often they are kept at the most basic level and have a lot of unstated assumption associated with them. Whilst they are not necessarily wrong, they definitely have to be treated very critically if you intend to use them.

Note that questions of validity are quite different from two people disagreeing about the definition of a concept: some of us, for example, would define 'democracy' procedurally (involving free elections, a free press, legitimate opposition, etc.) while others would draw more on a substantive definition (emphasizing that it has to express the will of the people, define how to draw boundaries vis-à-vis undemocratic parties, some measure of substantive equality, etc.); such a discussion does not reflect a problem of validity but of conceptual substance (Adcock and Collier 2001). Once one of us defined the concept in a particular way, validity asks whether—to use the first conception of democracy—free elections and the like are a good indicator of that type of democracy. The philosophical issue preceding the conceptual debate is important but not directly related to turning an idea into an observable implication.

How, then, would you know if an indicator or observation was valid? Whatever else you do, rely on your *common sense* first: if something walks like a duck and talks like a duck, it probably is a duck (and therefore best cooked with oranges ☺). The flip side is never to blindly adopt someone else's operationalization of a concept: you can use their measures, of course, but for reasons of your own. IQ tests may or may not be good ways of measuring intelligence, but using them simply because everyone else does is *not* intelligent. Sheep flock and investment bankers herd; social scientists think. Check for *robustness* where possible. If you are convinced that a concept can be measured in more than one way, then measure it in different ways: if you are right, you will discover high correlations between the two measurements. (This assumes, of course, that the two measures are independent of each other, or else you would be measuring the same thing twice.) *Use your imagination*: sometimes you cannot measure the concept directly, but you can measure its consequences. For example, it is impossible to measure if teachers (yes, *teachers*—read on) cheat on central final-year exams such as the French *Baccalauréat*, British A-levels, or the German *Abitur*. But, as Levitt (2005) reports in *Freakonomics*, you can run a check on the pattern of mistakes in each teacher's class; since they only have a short time between collecting the exams and handing them over to the central markers, cheats have to act quickly, and they show a high frequency of the same errors interspersed with the same correct answers, while the results of the others will be more random. (Teachers cheat, in Levitt's story, because their pay is related to the results of their students—you can, just perhaps, over-incentivize...). In the 1960s, a marvellous book entitled *Unobtrusive Measures* (Webb 1966) came out which discussed loads of ways of measuring things that may not be all that easy to find out (one of my favourites is the sudden increase in water consumption during commercial breaks as an indicator of a particular TV programme's popularity). Think of data in terms of the *relevance to their context*: concepts, like jokes, cannot be assumed to travel easily across different cultures (Locke and Thelen 1995; Adcock and Collier 2001: 535 ff.). The words 'political party', for example, do not mean the same thing in continental Europe, with its many, often ideological parties, the United Kingdom with its very few leadership parties, and the United States, where parties are perhaps best thought of as loose pre-electoral government coalitions. Party membership may therefore well have to be thought of in different ways in these three cases. And, finally, when doing interviews, *ask the interviewees* how they would think about a more or less abstract concept; since practically all will have at least a high-school and often university degree, they are likely to know what you are talking about, and they may have some ideas. Remember, though, that interviewees are not oracles (one of John's problems). While often you can take on face value what your interviewees tell you, be aware that people are brilliant rationalizers. If someone in a company tells you (as happened to me) that they saw the problem coming all along and that they then took the bull by the horns, you can be sure, if you know that the company faced a rather unexpected crisis just from looking at their results over those years and that it took them a long time to turn the company around, that the advantage of hindsight may have turned into a disadvantage.

Reliability, the second test that statements about the world need to pass, deals with the issue of how stable your measurement is. If a thermometer measures a hot day as 30°C on Monday and the same heat, according to the weather report, as 35°C on Tuesday, it is considered unreliable. The same in your research: reliability means that if you apply the same procedure for measuring something, you will end up with the same result if nothing else has changed that could influence that (King et al. 1994: 25). There are two ways to handle this, and combining them is not a bad idea. The first one is that you try to repeat the question, coding, or whatever means of operationalizing concepts you used. If all went well, you should arrive with the same answer, value, or general outcome. But be aware that people do not like to be asked the same thing twice or confronted with inconsistencies in their answers.

The second way is that you ask, where possible, someone else to repeat the question for you. Studies that rely on other sources, such as panels of experts (people who have to assign a value to a particular situation or event), always have at least two people translate this diffuse qualitative material into one-dimensional numerical codes between, say, 1 and 5. Think back to the example on the centre of political gravity on a Left/ Right scale that I mentioned earlier: you ask more than one person to score parties on that scale and discuss inconsistencies with the judges as a way of pinning down where parties are. It is customary to check (and report) the basic statistics between the judges' scores: even if the correlations are strong, large standard deviations may suggest that the scale used is perhaps not as one-dimensional as you thought. This type of checking for reliability can even happen in a very informal and *ex post* way, for instance when you meet someone at a conference who is working in the same area as you are; use the inevitable swapping of interview stories as a way of checking your interpretations against your conversation partner's.

Replicability, the third and final criterion, is in essence not much more than a call to intellectual honesty: explain how you moved from concept to operationalization so that anyone can replicate your research and check your results. In practical terms, this comes down to giving as much information when presenting data-sets as someone else would need to reproduce the data-set: say how you coded variables or had them coded (and how often), and how you dealt with inconsistencies. The basic idea is related to reliability, but this time from the point of view of the method rather than the outcome in terms of data: when you rely on data that you collected to develop a narrative that underpins your argument, you give the reader a clear idea of how you got to these data, so that he or she can then replicate the method. Telling them how you coded variables in a data-set, for example, allows other researchers—who might disagree with you, and probably will or at least try to if they are serious—to redo the analysis the way you did, or in a slightly different way, and to assess how robust your results were.

While replicability is relatively easy to assure in the case of quantitative data, it is highly complicated in more discursive research settings, where the data literally do not exist without your interpretation. When you are going through archives and newspaper reports, or especially when you rely on interviews, there are, so to speak, no data without you making them such by systematizing, ordering, and reporting them. In instances where you rely on external existing sources such as newspaper articles or archives, the problem is far from insurmountable: give the exact location of the source, stay close to the text, and then say what you made of it. Others can then, if they wish, go to the archive or call up the piece in an internet newspaper archive and check for themselves if you reported correctly. Not doing so—for example by lifting statements out of context—gets historians (and political scientists who rely on historical sources) in serious trouble, and rightly so.

With interviews, these things are different: unless you are willing to make your interview notes or tape transcripts publicly available (and assuming that the interviewee agrees with that), no one is looking over your shoulder. Replicability becomes deeply problematic in such cases. The best advice here is not to rely on interviews for data collection, but (*a*) to treat interviews as a means to try out ideas, get new ideas and (*b*) whenever you hear something in an interview that looks like you, would like to use it, find an alternative publicly available source that directly corroborates or indirectly supports the statement that you are relying on. On its own, the reference to an interview simply is not good enough. No one necessarily mistrusts you, but no one has to trust you blindly. (You can obviously use interview cites to spice up your story, as long as the key data are accessible elsewhere.) I can think of only one valid exception to this rule, and that is when you have privileged access without which the material would not exist. This is never a good situation to be in for the reasons outlined above, but if you are, so be it. The important thing then is to give sufficient background information that corroborates and contextualizes the information obtained in the interview to allow the readers to make up their own mind.

These three indicators of data quality–validity, reliability, and replicability—are mutually independent, but failing any of their implied tests is likely to cause problems for you at the thesis defence. While the problems appear on the whole more surmountable in quantitative research, they may seem intractable in research that relies on softer data and more interpretation. But the cavalry is, as I suggested earlier, never far away: the simple technique of *data triangulation* makes sure that even in 'soft' settings of data-gathering such as interviews, where a lot relies on subjective understanding on both sides of the interview, validity, reliability, and replicability meet minimum standards. The basic rule is to corroborate whatever you find with empirical material or data that measures the same thing from alternative, public sources, or the implications of what you heard. I will come back to this later in this chapter when I discuss interviews and archives in more detail. Let us first have a look at data which were prepared for you in public databases, and which often form the basis for quantitative studies. As we will see, issues of validity and reliability take on very strange forms there.

Public databases

Quantitative data gathered and made available by large public and quasi-public institutions such as national statistics offices, Eurostat, the OECD, the IMF, and the United Nations have become considerably more easily available since the Second World War and especially since the generalized adoption of internet sites by those organizations. You can now find out, often until very recently, what has happened in the world captured by those statistics: as recently as a few years ago for most, but even a few months or weeks in the case of statistics on the economy. Usually these statistics are pretty self-explanatory, especially to those who work in the sub-discipline: there is no mystery in what the number of cars or telephones per 1,000 inhabitants measures and very little in the case of GDP per capita. Things get a bit hairier perhaps for those outside economics and political economy when it comes to 'trade balance in current prices', but for those in the field it has the same transparency as the first straightforward indicators. Precisely because these statistics have a WYSIWYG quality to them ('what you see is what you get', an expression popularized in the early days when computers were spreading and what you typed on the screen was not necessarily what came out on the page), most of us do not spend too much time thinking about them, and start using them.

Many of these databases, however, may well have serious problems. Have a look at the data in Table 4.1. I invented them for didactic purposes (and to avoid having to hire a libel lawyer after having attributed them to any of these international organizations), but the example is not far-fetched. The figures in Table 4.1 report GDP growth in 2002 in five major advanced capitalist economies as reported by a trustworthy source such as the EU, the OECD, the World Bank, etc. (GDP is best thought of as the sum total of all economic activity in a given territory, expressed in a standard unit of value.) The first column presents the growth rate in 2002 that was reported as soon as figures became available in 2003, and in the second the growth rates as they were reported in 2006. What do you notice? Easy: every single one of these figures was adjusted slightly to reflect better measurement with the benefit of distance and more correct accounting. The relative order of the columns is exactly the same: United States and United Kingdom on top, France and Germany one order of magnitude below that, and Japan at the end. Since the order has not changed all that much, and the adjustments never involved more than 0.3 per cent, the difference between the two passes unnoticed. But spend a minute more by taking a careful second look: in the cases of Germany, the United Kingdom, and the United States, the 2003 data were almost one-tenth 'wrong' compared to the supposedly more accurate 2006 data: the German estimate was corrected by 0.2 per cent, and both the UK and the US estimates had a correction of 0.3 per cent. In the 2003 data, the US growth rate was also twice as high as the German one, whereas in the 2006 data the difference had fallen to (3.5 minus 2.1 and then divided by 2.1) two-thirds of the German figure; admittedly still a respectable difference but considerably less dramatic than the initial double. The difference between France and the United Kingdom, almost a full percentage point in 2003, has dwindled to half a percentage point by 2006.

Now think of what this might imply. Let us define annual GDP growth first. It is a fraction that has the following components: the difference between the GDP for the current year and the GDP of the

Table 4.1 GDP growth in four major economies, 2002, as reported in 2003 and 2006

	2003 figures	2006 figures
France	2.3	2.4
Germany	1.9	2.1
United Kingdom	3.2	2.9
United States	3.8	3.5
Japan	0.7	0.8

previous year, which is then divided by the GDP for the previous year in order to get the rate of growth. In these data, this is the GDP for 2002 minus the GDP for 2001, divided by the GDP for 2001: $(GDP_{2002}-GDP_{2001})/GDP_{2001}$. Small corrections of the sort in Table 4.1 can therefore have several sources: either the GDP for 2001 was overestimated or underestimated, the GDP for 2002 was underestimated or overestimated, or both were—the GDP for 2001 could have been underestimated by more (or less) than the GDP for 2002. Most of these corrections are usually just given in a new edition of the figures without much explanation (e.g. I have never seen a small note on such data corrections in OECD or World Bank figures), and many people just glance over them. But these data have real consequences. All other things being equal, I'd rather live in a country where the GDP in the 2003 edition underestimated both than in one where only the 2001 GDP was underestimated. But I would also prefer to live in a country that had the optimism of the United States and the United Kingdom in 2003, when they saw the first edition of the figures, and not in gloomy Germany.

For some indicators, such a correction matters more than for others. The data that Levitt (2005) used in his famous study relating the dramatic drop in violent crime in the early 1990s to the legalization of abortion in the United States during the 1970s may be off by a few points, but the general idea holds regardless of the actual values, since they are of the same order of magnitude and explain a lot more and more systematically than any other possible cause for the decline. But in the case of policies that are adopted as a result of economic underperformance, such small differences can have large effects, both in the academic debates that surround them and in the political debates that act upon them.

The main problem with such public databases is that we often do not even know what a reasonable correction factor should be. Take the dark number in crime, for example—the unrecorded cases of a crime which are not known. When you do not report that someone stole your bicycle, you are producing a dark number. When a man hits his wife (or vice versa) and he or she does not report it to the police, the same happens. And when the grocery store does not catch teenage confectionery thieves after school but simply lives with that by slightly raising the price of what is sold to paying customers, the store owner contributes to the dark number problem. With the exception of murder, which usually does not pass unnoticed or misreported—which is why Levitt (2005) concentrated on that—crime statistics are hardly ever useful for the purposes of social and political analysis. The dark number is usually not even a systematic underestimation that we can correct for: the 'real' number of rapes, one of the most under-reported crimes because of the stigma associated with it, might rise or fall, but you would not necessarily know this from looking at rape statistics. Apparently rape numbers jumped up several hundred per cent in the mid-1980s. Something in the water? The inadvertent effects of Mrs Thatcher's harsh economic policies? Hardly: instead, the police had started to encourage victims to come forward and prosecutors to proceed with cases. A rise in such figures might then depend on a growing awareness among the police that some reports involve rape where previously they would not have defined it like that, on the popularity of a TV programme that raised the issue, or because rape victims demonstrate in public and thus make it more legitimate for others to do so as well (as was probably the case with child abuse over the last decades). But the point is that on the whole we do not know if the underlying 'actual' number has shifted at all, and in which direction.

When using official statistics and public databases, remember that they were often constructed with a different goal in mind than the one you are using them for, and by people who were using definitions that may have been different from yours. In a classic study of strikes, Eric Batstone and his colleagues (1978) came up with an interesting discovery. In the 1970s in Britain, strikes were reported by employers to the national statistics office on a standard sheet that included rubrics along the lines of 'from when to when did the strike last', 'how many workers were on strike', and 'what was the cause of the strike'. There is nothing wrong *per se* with having employers report strikes, as far as I can tell: after all, they are a concerned party, and they can count and listen as well as anyone else. But Batstone and his team discovered that employers thought of the problem in a remarkable way: they first assessed what the cause of the strike was, and then filled in the other rubrics on the sheet. And sometimes employers decided that a stoppage by workers was not really a strike because it was legitimate in their eyes, while another was because they considered it less justified. For example, in one instance workers go on strike to support their claim for higher wages. The employer duly notes that, fills in the sheet, and sends it to the statistics office. But when workers strike because an old machine that should have been replaced was not, and has injured several of their colleagues over the last few months, things begin to move. The employer assesses the reason for the strike, vows to replace the machine, and does not send back the sheet: in the eyes of the employer, there was no illegitimate reason to stop work-ing, and the action could therefore not be called a strike (it is important to know that British companies have, in contrast to many of their European counterparts, no institutionalized forms of workers' participa-tion that would have picked up this faulty machine long before it became a death trap). Unsurprisingly, UK strike statistics in the 1970s almost invariably reported that workers went on strike for higher wages; the truth is that we will never know if they did or not, since we do not know how many faulty machines, draughty workplaces, dangerous substances, and obnoxious lower managers were at the basis of the stoppages that were never reported.

In the limiting case, two official statistics purporting to measure the same thing may even contradict each other. A classic example of the latter is that the unemployment rate reported by the German officials is always higher than the standardized rate calculated by the OECD, while in the United Kingdom the situation is the other way around. For the first few years of the 2000s, the United Kingdom has had a self-reported un-employment rate of about 5 per cent, and Germany one of about 9 per cent. A big difference that warrants some careful looking into and pos-sibly even dramatic labour market reforms. The OECD standardized rates, however, show a slightly different picture: the UK's unemployment rate jumps to 6.5 per cent, while Germany's falls below 8 per cent. That is a considerably less dramatic difference than we thought at first, which could be explained by many things other than the dynamism of the UK economy.

These examples throw up the notion of comparability of official statis-tics. Clearly Germany and the United Kingdom do not measure their unemployment rates in the same way, and fortunately the OECD corrects for that by imposing a uniform definition. But sometimes that is not done. Say that out of concern for rising social exclusion and xenophobia, you want to find out the rate of foreign nationals in jails (this example was given to me by Nicola Lacey, for which my thanks). You could give the absolute numbers for different countries, but that does not tell you all that much, really, since (all other things being equal) large countries may have more foreign nationals than small countries. So, at the very least you need to link that to the presence of these nationalities in the population as a whole. However, since it is not clear if only foreign passport holders or also second and third generation immigrants are treated as foreign nationals in official statistics across different countries (some do and others do not), how do you standardize your numbers? In addition, the definition of 'imprisonment' is not the same everywhere either: are people in 'administrative' detention centres (i.e. those who have not been judged and probably will never be) included? And what about juveniles who are in homes rather than jails? Unless all countries in your study have similar judicial practices and similar ways of reporting on those, you are likely to end up with data that are not going to allow you to say much across different cases.

Official statistics, as all of this suggests, should come with a severe health warning, even when they are supposedly standardized and comparable. Most official and public databases have or should have a section on how they were compiled; carefully read those, regardless of your plans with the data, but definitely if you plan to use them for sophisticated statistical analysis. If in doubt, ask the statistical offices for a succinct statement of the methodology. Table 4.2 summarizes this discussion by listing the most important pitfalls in official statistics and how to check for them. But the morale of this story is clear: when someone else does the work, you can never be sure that the data are as clean as you ideally would like them to be. This is not a matter of deliberately misleading the public (although that has happened, as we now discover with output statistics of the Soviet economies) or of incompetence; it is often a relatively innocent consequence of why and how the data were collected. Critiquing the data by confronting them with other official sources may sometimes work, but not always, and then you have to get your hands a lot dirtier than you thought you would. Think of the strike statistics example earlier: Batstone and his colleagues could only find out that there was a problem with the official strike statistics by doing old-fashioned field research that allowed them to deconstruct the reporting method and the implicit judgements that were used in them. In the end nothing beats constructing your own data—or by extension using data that someone else constructed but with similar research aims as you have.

Table 4.2 Checklist for official statistics

- Check the data in different editions over several years:
  - How large are the corrections?
  - Does it make sense to use averages over several years?
- Check other official statistics: do the data go in the same direction or do they contradict each other?
- Check the methodology of the database:
  - How were the data reported?
  - Who did the reporting?
  - Was the reporting consistent and monitored?
- Can you estimate the nature of the dark number? Can you find out if it is consistent across observations?
- Are data comparable across cases (countries, sectors, regions, etc.)?

Constructing your own data and database

One of the big differences between, for example, sociologists and other more micro-oriented social scientists, on the one hand, and political scientists and political economists on the other, is that the latter very often take data produced by someone else at face value, while the former to a large extent consider it necessary to collect data themselves. Between these two extremes, a simple rule emerges when it comes to handling data: *get as close to the production of the data as you can.* Find out who collected the data, how they did it, for whom, etc. Do not assume that a national statistical office necessarily does everything right, or that it does not matter if tobacco producers collect material on the effects of smoking instead of the Health Ministry. If the informal economy covers as much as an estimated 25 per cent of GDP, the officially reported GDP figures may be pretty much useless, but you would not know that from a national statistical office.

Getting close to the production of the data allows you to discover the underlying biases in the data, their weaknesses and strengths, and then the gaps in the data. After such a stock-taking exercise, you can try and reconstruct data, see how the holes might be filled, and what you need to do to safeguard the integrity of the data you've been using. Remember also that aggregate data may hide tremendous variation: for example, two countries may be equally wealthy when expressed in GDP per capita. But one of them may have a very compressed income structure, while the other is highly unequal. Knowing this allows you to think about whether this matters at all for you, and—more interestingly, perhaps—may put you on track to define an interesting research question.

When working with aggregate data, the simplest and definitely among the most reliable sources are databases (web sites or depositories) which have been organized by colleagues, and the list serves and web discussion groups that are often associated with these public resources or with the topics they cover. This is one of the few truly inestimable blessings of the internet for research: you can use those networks to ask individual researchers for their data, how they got them, how they used them, and if anyone knows where they might be or how to resolve problems you encounter (you might be interested to know that this was standard practice already in the late Middle Ages and especially during the Renaissance, when scientists from all over Europe exchanged views—in Latin—about research problems; the internet has finally taken us back there—in English). The main reason why such data are useful for you is that they have usually been cleaned up, and researchers usually tell you how they did that, why, and what they were trying to do with the data. Even if they rely on official statistics, these have been reorganized to become research tools rather than management or policy instruments. Moreover, if the data-set covers more countries, cross-national comparability has become one of the main concerns of such researchers. If your and their goals overlap, these data are ready for almost immediate consumption. However, since there is, as far as I know, no central place where you can find out who has which data available, the fastest way to find out is often to contact the researchers indirectly (via their web site) or directly to ask for their data-sets.

Aggregate data have their limits, though. Not only could they mask significant internal variation, they are not particularly good at presenting dynamics—logically so, since they are considered to be summary statistics. Take labour productivity, for example: imagine an economy with two equally sized companies, in which A makes high value-added goods, and where hourly labour productivity is, say, 150, while B is concentrating on cost-competitive segments, and has a labour productivity level, say, of 50. The aggregate (i.e. average) productivity level of the economy is 100, but the way company A makes its products is likely to be very different from the way company B will do so. All other things being equal, company A is likely to spend more on R&D, skills and training, and wages, while also having more participative management structures. These two companies thus seem to belong in two different types of sub-economies, but the aggregate figure would not tell you anything about that. Only when you go and find out how these aggregate data were constructed can you tell. Something like this happened in Italy in the 1970s and early 1980s, when researchers discovered that there were more or less informal dynamic networks of small firms in particular regions (the 'Third Italy') which outperformed their large-firm neighbours, and quite easily managed to stave off international competition (Bagnasco 1977).

Dealing with such problems is not always simple. When I was an undergraduate student in sociology, we were trained in designing survey questionnaires with closed questions (as opposed to the open questions that have been at the basis of most of the other interviews discussed in this chapter) which gave us as good as complete control over the collection of data. That was a hard learning school, and quite a few of the first drafts of these questionnaires required at least another four or five versions to be workable—so be aware, if you intend to do a survey, that the first draft of your questionnaire is not nearly going to be as good as you would ideally want it to be. Always have these things read by colleagues, and if possible test them on a small sample of the population to see if they understand the question the way you intended, and if the data over the entire sample, including combinations of questions that you had designed, are as straightforward to interpret as you thought. But if designed well, surveys are a good way to collect data. Surveys, however, also use a set of working assumptions, which you need to be aware of: remember that once you start working with the data, the individual responses disappear and these data take on a life of their own. Getting them straight is therefore crucial.

The most important problems with survey data are relatively simple to see, even for an outsider. One is that you assume that the *respondents mean what they say*. This is probably not much of a problem when you ask them how their working day is structured, but that may be quite a different story when you ask about income or sex life. The second is that the questions are *understood the way you meant them to be*. Again, this probably is not all that difficult when you ask them what time they go to bed and when they get up. However, once you start using scales (of the 'agree strongly–agree–neither agree nor disagree, etc.' type) to ask them what type of meaning they attached to when they went to bed or got up, you are imposing a response structure on the people you interview which may not be the one they would use to give meaning to these activities. This can become especially problematic when you have cross-national surveys: a straightforward question in English can become a hornet's nest in French because of two related reasons. The first one is that a literal translation of a phrase in English might not mean all that much to a French person; but by paraphrasing and contextualizing the question, you may end up trapped in a validity problem, since you have changed, however slightly, the measurement as you intended it. The second, more important one, is known as the *anchor problem*. Imagine that you are doing a survey on corruption in politics (the example was given to me by Herbert Kitschelt). When we ask people in one country on how high they estimate corruption, we assume that they mean the same thing. A simple example, can illustrate this: when an Italian has to judge corruption, he or she might well say that a particular activity is quite OK, and 'Italy' might score lower in international comparisons than Sweden, because a Swedish respondent would find the same activity far more corrupt. Does this mean that Sweden has suddenly become a breeding ground for corrupt politicians? Probably not; instead it is very likely that Swedish respondents have a much higher standard to begin with, while Italian respondents consider many activities in shadowy areas not really all that much beyond the law. Finally, be aware that there's a *difference* between what people say they think about something and what they will actually do about it. If you ask someone if they would buy a good or a service if it were made available, they would almost certainly answer that positively—but you might be in for a surprise if you then actually introduce the service; your question was, in effect, couched in implicit *ceteris paribus* terms, but the world does not operate in such terms. Most of these problems with survey research are well known, and there is even a whole branch of statistics and survey research that tries to devise ways to correct for these. Whenever you think about using a survey as a means of data collection, at the very least consider what the problems might be, and have a careful look at how others have dealt with such issues.

One final but important warning. Be aware that gathering information by asking people about their lives, either in the structured interview settings that we can find in survey research, or when relying on open questions, may involve serious ethical issues. If you are interested in such heavily emotionally laden subjects as child abuse or rape, you may face the horrible dilemma of asking very hurting questions and obtain (let us assume) excellent data, or have a more tactful way of dealing with your interviewees at the risk of lower quality of the material. No one knows if the supposed good that you may do with your research outweighs the pain you may cause, but don't ignore the choices. Often you can rely on your supervisors, doctoral programme representatives, or a university code on ethics in research to help you think through if and how your research may have problematic ethical facets. Find out what they say, and then see how your research measures up against that. While closing your eyes to these issues may get you a strong reputation, it may not be the one that you want to grow old with.

Pillaging public sources or conducting surveys are a common way to collect data. But often this cannot be done: the question does not allow for such structured data collection since there are too many potential causes to find out about, there are too many unpredictable things going on in the broad area that you are interested in, or the money simply is not available. Alternatives are at hand, but not without a cost: structured and semistructured interviews, and archival and other written sources are among the most widely used but, methodologically, possibly also among the most complicated techniques of producing your data in the social sciences. Often these techniques fit quite nicely with the premises of a configurational approach: you try to assess many complex interactions at the same time, let your sources and interviewees speak for themselves and in their own words, and you explore the implications with them by connecting the dots between individual points. Whilst such sources allow you to correct for the types of problems that haunt standardized surveys, they open up more than one other can of methodological worms.

Interviews, data, and triangulation

If validity is a central concern in the use of official statistics, reliability and replicability are the main problems that haunt case study-based research designs. Validity matters here as well, of course, but the most important issue is how to work so that someone else who is doing your research would see your material in more or less the same way? Think for a moment of the setting in which you are operating: an interview usually involves you and one person or a very small number of people, the door is closed, the interview takes the form of a conversation, and you are taking notes while it happens (or record the interview on tape and take notes afterwards). Nobody else is there, and the interview cannot simply be reproduced by sending in someone else with the same list of open questions that you used. Assuming that you more or less know what you are looking for and that what you find more or less covers what you want to find out (the problem of validity), you are then faced with the problem of having to convince a professionally sceptic audience of other scholars. The answer to this is quite simple: avoid having to rely on interview data alone. Triangulate the insights you obtained during the interview with material that supports what you found. If you do interviews with officials or company managers, there are usually public sources against which you can check what someone told you. This form of data triangulation (not to be confused with methodological triangulation whereby you subject the same question to different ways of answering it) works on the principle of iteration. You corroborate your interviews with other, independent, material: other interviews, research reports, annual reports, newspaper articles, etc. The purpose of the interview is then less to find the silver bullet, but to collect insights and pieces of information that you can match to other pieces of information, which together make up a convincing story.

Interviewing is, like so many things in the social sciences, a skill that you learn by doing. All of us with some experience in this will remember some of our first interviews that went horribly wrong, and there is no foolproof guarantee that it will not go wrong again. Developing a good interview technique is akin to learning how to drive a car: you may pass your driving test, sure, but we all know that becoming a good driver is a matter of years after that, and the same is true for interviews. Basically, there are three dimensions to keep in mind: when to interview, whom, and how?

When to interview? The golden rule is to start interviews when you are ready for them, else they may turn into a waste of time for you and the interviewee. That does not necessarily mean that you have to wait until you have all your hypotheses ready for testing. Interviews will force you to revise these, so earlier is often better than later. Just make sure you know what you are talking about. It is usually quite a good idea to use interviews early on in your research to narrow your topic, gather insights that you had not anticipated, and then use that material to prepare the next interviews. My experience is that you can often get a good sense of the validity of your approach and basic hunches after one or two interviews. Rely on that information for what follows: sharpen the next interviews on the basis of those insights, start entertaining new ideas, and write down what you think you learnt from the interview as soon as you can (on the train or plane home, with a cup of coffee in a café afterwards, or in your hotel room). When interviewing with two or more (although three really should be the maximum, lest it begins to look like the Spanish Inquisition or, worse, an exam board), always spend some time debriefing as soon as you can after the interview. You and your colleague(s) may have picked up different things from the interview, and that information should not be lost.

Who to interview? Start with a wish list of the people you would ideally like to talk to. If you're interviewing people in large organizations, go for the top and work your way down from there. A letter from your supervisor or teacher may help getting you access if that is difficult: they can write something along the lines of 'a research project is underway at university X, and we would appreciate it if you gave our researcher some of your time'. Always consider if these are the right people for the kind of information you need. Specialized interviewees (e.g. lawyers or engineers) do not necessarily know much outside their immediate area of expertise, so it is usually more useful to talk to them later on in the process, when you also know more about this area. Since others that you could interview may have a broader perspective on an issue, calibrate interviews accordingly.

Try to think of people who might have a different view (e.g. managers *and* unionists, or different sides of a policy issue)? Interview those as well: as you know from making up after rows with your loved ones, there is often more than one plausible interpretation of a tense situation.

How to interview? One hour is a long time for busy people: prepare interviews well. But don't over-prepare. Make sure you ask all the questions you need to ask. Get purely factual things out of the way early in the interview (How big is your budget? What kinds of products do you make? . . .). Do not stick religiously to the order in a list of questions; a 'discussion' with the interviewee, in which you challenge what they just said can often get you more interesting insights (in order to avoid unnecessary friction, I recommend using expressions such as 'If I may play the devil's advocate for a moment' to introduce such challenges). The order of the questions can vary; make sure you know which ones you've asked and which ones are still to come. When doing interviews with a colleague, alternate taking notes and checking questions.

Ask questions with the interviewee's words, and as much as possible in the interviewee's world. However, even though they are not working on a doctorate, they are not idiots either, so sometimes, if you are clear enough about what you are doing, asking (almost) the exact question you are asking yourself can do wonders, because they may completely understand what you mean, and you can then explore lower levels of abstraction afterwards with them. Remember also that you start with a big advantage: most interviewees are truly flattered that someone in academia is interested in what they are doing, and are usually very positively predisposed. (And if they are not at the start, things can change during the interview for the same reason: an engineer responsible for quality control in a large French company started an interview in a somewhat awkward way by incredulously asking me why someone doing a Ph.D. at MIT would be interested in his job. Once he understood that I knew what I was talking about and after I had explained what the issue was I was trying to understand, he lightened up tremendously and I got a lot of good material out of that interview.) My strategy is usually to tell them in a few minutes and in the language you would use for your grandmother (*remember?*) what I'm doing in the project and then ask them what they do in relation to that topic or a particular question. After a few minutes the ice is broken and you can then politely intervene and ask them more details, or link what they've just said to the questions you are asking.

Finally, be fair towards your interviewees. Lay down early what the ground rules regarding attribution and especially literal citation are. Many would want (and have the right!) to know what you make of their words when you write them up. Respect people when they say that they do not want to talk about something. Remember that you will be talking to others, and one of them might be more willing to raise the thorny issue. Stop the interview by asking two questions: the first is what they would like to say that has not been said during the interview; the second who else they would recommend inside or outside the organization for an interview. Explicitly ask if you can use their name when contacting these people.

Conclusion

Data are crucial in any empirical research project. The central questions when it comes to data follow logically from what was discussed earlier in this book: how are your data related to the question you are asking, what type of data will you be using, and do you have access to them? Can you critically examine the data, and will they allow you to examine what you want to? Data, of any kind, are therefore intrinsically problematic: official statistics have their pitfalls, cleaned-up databases do not always exist or are not always easily accessible, and constructing your own data from scratch is not always possible. Interviews and archives, the budget options for many of us, are riddled with their own problems, primarily those of reliability and replicability. In the end, how well you use your empirical material, hard data or otherwise, is your own work. You may have to think about slightly more roundabout ways of measuring what you are interested in, and you will have to consider how to triangulate data; but even then there may remain a shadow of arbitrariness in your research. The consolation is that if you have tried to do things right when moving from concept to operationalization, if you say how you did that, and if your data shed light on an interesting dimension of an interesting question, you will receive the benefit of the doubt. In themselves, data don't say anything: they become relevant as a result of your question, and they are treated as what they are in light of the answers you are giving. And that cannot be resolved by data; that is a matter of how you integrate the empirical data with the rest of your project. Data become data, as it were, when you use them as a way of engaging an argument and write them up.

FURTHER READING TO CHAPTER 4

One of the central discussions among methodologists these days is about measurement validity. Adcock and Collier (2001) summarize that debate quite well and offer some intelligent commentary on the many ways that concepts and data interact. Webb (1966) discuss proxy data and other ways of 'unobtrusive' measuring. Huff (1991) goes through the many ways that statistics can obscure instead of enlighten our understanding of the world. Block (1990) shows how many statistics for OECD countries fail to capture basic economic dynamics and the implications of this. Hamilton (1996) discusses the weak empirical evidence for key theories in the social sciences (Weber's *Protestant Ethic* and the middle-class voters for Hitler receive a particularly hard beating). Finally, all this attention to data has come under fire from postmodernist authors. Whilst I have my doubts about much of this work, Foucault's *The Order of Things: An Archaeology of the Human Sciences* (1970) is a magisterial critique of what social science is. Bruno Latour's *Science in Action* (1987) is another intelligent analysis on the production of data in science in general.

5 Writing Up Your Research

Everyone who teaches graduate students probably recognizes the following scene, if not from our own graduate experience, then definitely from our years as a teacher. Ask any third- or fourth-year doctoral student how far they've got in their research and there is a big chance that you receive an answer along the lines of 'I have finished my field research and am now beginning to write it up. I hope to finish a draft in the next six months and submit my thesis in about a year.' Ask the same student again a year later, and you are bound to receive a very similar answer. Has this student truly done nothing in between? Very unlikely. What has probably happened is something else. The student has discovered that *producing* your research—asking the right question, collecting material, and interpreting it in a way that it sheds new light on the issue—is something very different from *reproducing* your research on paper. Unfortunately, since the thesis is ultimately what they are judged on, there is no short cut. The student almost certainly also discovered that more empirical research was needed, not in the general, almost ubiquitous sense that students always claim that they need to do more research, but in the practical sense that when they started writing up, they discovered there were holes in their material in light of the argument they were making.

In the social sciences, our pen (or laptop keyboard if the image of a pen is too retro for you) is by and large the only tool that we have for telling others about the work that we do. Unless research is written up, it does not exist. You will get helpful hints and 'well done' pats on the shoulder from your supervisors and others you talk to about your research, but your name is not (yet) associated with an idea until it exists on paper. Since common modesty suggests that you are probably not the only one to come up with an idea (simply accept that if you can think it, there is nothing to stop someone else from thinking it), there are two possible reactions to this conundrum. The first one is unfortunately all too common: students begin to live the life of an intellectual hermit, guard their material jealously, and withdraw or politick when they discover that others are inching towards their insight in order to stop them from finding out what they think they were the first to see. The other response is considerably healthier: start writing. Writing forces you to be clear about argument and structure, invites comments that ought to help you in your research as it develops, puts you on the map, and indicates very directly where more work is needed so that you can economize your resources to finish the project in a satisfactory way. 'Don't get it right,' is Peter Hall's highly sensible advice (1990) to senior Ph.D. researchers, 'get it written'.

The fastest way to get to this stage, and possibly the only way to avoid the need-more-research trap, is to start writing early—papers first and very early on, sections of the thesis afterwards, and the whole thing in the last stage. One of the more humbling experiences in my life was the comment on one of my first essays, a twenty-page single-spaced examination of theories on revolutions: 'A very thoughtful essay. Next time, you might want to think about making an argument.' Writing a paper, I discovered, is a skill. Thoughts are important, but structure, explicit logic, and organization are equally important. You can learn many skills—and this one in particular—by doing. And one of the best ways is to present your written work, in small groups of research students, in departmental seminars, and, as time goes by, in conferences. Ask everyone for critical comments, and if one of them suggests that with some revisions the paper you wrote might be publishable, talk to your supervisor(s) about sending it off to a good journal. In short, use the writing apprenticeship as a way of honing your research, acquiring skills, and building a portfolio and a relevant research environment for the things you want to do.

This chapter starts with the more abstract problem of the logical criteria that a paper, or, in fact, any written work, would have to pass. That section embeds the process of writing up your research in the discussions on research design that this book has developed since the first chapter. I then discuss how to get down to the notebook and write good research papers (including which mistakes to avoid at all cost), and finish with a section on how to extend that when writing a thesis.

Rules of logic to help you write

As a rule, the structure of your paper or book should reflect the design of your research and not the process of your research. Readers are, with a few exceptions such as your partner, not all that interested in how you obtained the insights and knowledge you present, but in how well you make your case. Your paper, dissertation, or thesis should have only one goal in mind: persuading the reader that you know what you are talking about, that you do it in a way that is interesting to read, and which reflects the logical (and not just the chronological) evolution of your research and argument.

There are, in the social sciences, two broad approaches to report on research: induction and deduction. Purely inductive research refers to research whereby the report assembles the facts you find in a way to make them accessible for others and then builds arguments on that basis. Much historical research is (or better, was) of this kind: imagine we would always have to go and delve into archives ourselves each time we refer to something that happened in the past. Having books on the subject—from the Peloponnese wars over the spread of Christianity and the rise of capitalism in the West to the fall of the Berlin Wall—makes life easy for us. Writing this up requires no more than being faithful to the material, that is, not to claim that things happened which you either cannot prove happened or which you know did not happen. However, since we are trying to make sense of what happened, both as writer and as reader, a simple and dry version of it all is not enough: there needs to be a beginning to the account, a middle, and something of an ending—the latter usually what needs to be explained. The deductive research tradition starts from the opposite idea: what are the theoretical implications of a few basic assumptions? Most 'serious' economics (and increasingly political science) today is of this type. The papers are usually built around a few core assumptions and a model—mathematical or not—to prove a point. For example, the organization of factories is divided into a few simple but relevant dimensions, and the author then shows that this division helps us understand other aspects of organizational behaviour which up until then were not part of the standard insights in the discipline. These types of papers also require a beginning, middle, and ending, but their purpose is not any longer to make a process intelligible, but to push the debate on the theoretical implications of a particular position.

Most work in the social sciences today falls between these two pure versions: most papers and books develop a logical argument, and then try and show how this argument works out in practice. Unfortunately, whereas the rules for writing up are relatively clear in the case of the two pure traditions, this is much less so for the majority of us. In *Analytical Narratives*, Bates (1998) suggest a way of dealing with this which is relevant for those who use a relatively formalized version of an argument as well as for those who are more 'historically' and empirically minded. In his piece he claims that any good research has to able to pass these five tests.

Test 1: Do the assumptions of a model, an argument, or a theory fit the facts as they are known? This may seem an obvious criterion to pass, but it is in fact not entirely unchallenged in political economy. When someone pointed out to Milton Friedman that his theory was elegant but contradicted basic fundamentals in human behaviour, he responded that the value of a theory was only its capacity to predict what was going to happen—even if it started by violating many 'known' facts. He was, in fact, not alone in that: much of the in-my-eyes trivial economics of today would be a lot better if it incorporated known facts about human behaviour instead of simply working its way through accepted, but obviously incorrect ideas about how humans respond.

The point is, especially in empirical political science, important: if we want to understand policies, the effects of institutions, or the changes in a political system under political or economic duress, we would do well to start from assumptions that are in line with what we know already. For example, a paper which evaluates the EU's social policy complaining that it should be an area for supranational decision-making, would do well to retry and understand why some (in fact most) issue areas are not of that kind in the EU. And those who want to understand the war in the former Yugoslavia would not help themselves if they started from the idea that Milosevic wanted a peaceful transition to a federation. Conversely, starting a paper on social policy in the EU with the premise that it is an intergovernmental area, or that Milosevic has a violent domestic agenda, would be on safer ground: if anyone disagreed with those assumptions, it should be relatively easy to rebut these objections.

Test 2: Do the conclusions follow from the premises? Again, a point that seems obvious in its simplicity—if a conclusion goes off on a tangent or contradicts the starting points for the analysis, it weakens the whole paper. Using the examples above, imagine that you started out with the assumption that Milosevic had a brutal domestic agenda; in that case it is not recommended to conclude that the Kosovo war was purely a provocation by NATO (note that it is irrelevant whether the war was or was not NATO'S fault, just do not contradict your initial premise).

How does one find out if conclusions follow from premises? When using more formal methods, that is relatively easy: depending on the degree of formalization, all that is necessary is to check the mathematics, or look at how outcomes reflect the basic underlying model of the method or theory. For more qualitatively organized research reports, however, it is important to make as explicit as possible what is being argued and what it means in its implications, so that you can set your data against that central argument and its implications in the clearest form. For example, if you argue that decentralized models of democratic decision-making are easier to implement in polities with a strong non-state component (or civil society, as it is called today), then you have to think through what forms state and non-state forms of social organization might take, and if degrees of associational organization make a difference.

If tragedy strikes despite all your precautions, that is, if your findings lead you to a conclusion that you had not anticipated, you will have to reframe the paper or thesis to make sure that the first and last part actually fit. One way of dealing with it is to be more explicit about the conditions under which your argument might and might not operate; another is to drop the pet argument altogether and develop something new that combines what you originally thought with the new ideas you have (in fact, most social science works like that, so that's no problem, but you may want to avoid discovering it while writing a paper or thesis).

Test 3: Do the implications of the argument find confirmation in the data? This rather trivial and seemingly obvious question is in fact a critical epistemological point. Your theory is not just there to be confirmed by the data; it is also a lens through which you look at the world and try to make it intelligible. This is what makes research so fascinating: your argument should predict what you will find, much in the same way (but with less precision) that astronomers know that there is a new planet out there on the basis of calculations and circumstantial evidence. This third question in effect blurs the conventional distinction between deduction and induction: if your data follow from your theory, they are not simply out there, but actively constructed by the theory.

What if the data and the argument conflict? As I pointed out before, there is no way around it: reframe the theory. But do not discard it. If you came up with it after long reflection, it must contain a grain of truth somewhere, and that means you should not simply get rid of it because you found one bit that doesn't work. Evaluate what might and might not work and specify better under which conditions it does.

Test 4: **How much better is your argument than other, competing explanations?** If a theory explains more variation within one case than another, then it is stronger. Parsimony is an important parameter to keep in mind here: say as much as possible with as few tools (words) as possible. However, sometimes more complex explanations can give you more leverage, since they explain dynamics that are ignored by other arguments. The general rule in selecting among theories is, in principle therefore, simple: choose the most powerful. Take the example of Daniel Goldhagen's famous book (1996) on German anti-semitism and the Holocaust. His project was to understand the Holocaust as a result of a form of 'eliminationist anti-semitism, with [...] hurricane-force potential, [which] resided ultimately in the heart of German political culture, in German society itself', and argues that the 'ubiquitous and profound hatred of the ghettoized Jews' by the German people which developed since the Middle Ages (Goldhagen 1996: 52 ff.), had over the centuries become 'integral to German culture' (Goldhagen 1996: 55). The Holocaust was, in other words, an element that had developed over several hundred years and permeated the German collective psyche by the late 1920s with the dramatic consequences that we know now. But there are more dynamic theories that you can develop about the Holocaust. Understanding the rise of the Nazis and the Holocaust as the contingent outcome of failing class coalitions, for example, or of how a crisis in the 1930s allowed these particular anti-semitic ideas to take root in a society that was infused with modern universalist notions of science, art, and politics, is probably more powerful. Such explanations can help us understand why Jews do not have to be afraid in Berlin today (or did not have to be before the First World War). Alternatively, you could try and understand what was special about German anti-semitism and what it shared with others (Birn and Riess 1997: 196) in order to understand how deep-seated this 'eliminationist anti-semitism' actually was. Since both of the alternatives incorporate more facts than Goldhagen's, they are better theories in the sense that Lakatos used the term.

Sometimes your theory is not the most powerful one, however, and then you face the problem of having to accept the other one, unless you are able to incorporate sources of variation in your argument which were not predicted by the other theories. In other words, if you build an argument at a more general level than where the competing explanations are located, you might be able to point out that the competing theory is a special case of your theory, or offers a partial explanation which needs to be complemented.

Test 5: How useful is the explanation for understanding or explaining other cases? Research has the ambition to say something about cases that were not studied; by implication the importance of your research therefore increases with the level of generalization of your propositions. Test 5 can therefore be seen as the ultimate test for linking actual research and research design to writing. Passing it can take many different forms. At the very least, an argument has to be able to make sense of another, but similarly structured case. For example, if you discover that in Germany the role of labour unions in industrial restructuring is important because they impose constraints on business that preclude the low-road option of lowering wages or firing large parts of the workforce, while offering the possibilities (through social peace, training policies, etc.) for business to reorganize, then it makes sense to look at Sweden or Belgium. Since labour unions supposedly have a similar role there as in Germany, things should more or less work out in the same way. You will then find that Belgium and Sweden indeed follow the same path as Germany. From a sophisticated causal mechanism that worked in one case, you developed a considerably wider argument which can now be tested against countries where labour unions are different. If your research design was sound, then it must have wider relevance for other cases, and it makes sense to bring that out in the concluding section of the paper or the thesis, because it bolsters your argument.

If the argument in a paper passes these five tests—is it realistic, logical, empirically grounded, better than competing explanations, and useful for understanding other cases?—you are on the way to conveying the logical structure of your research design into a paper that does your work justice.

Writing a paper

Now, how do you make these criteria work when you are facing a white sheet of paper or a blank computer screen? There is no secret to a paper, but there are four golden rules. (My colleague Nick Barr has sent these around to students for years and they summarize very well what is to follow. My advice is to print them out, frame them, and hang them over your desk next to the 'observable implications' sign from Chapter 1.) The paper you are writing should have a *structure* which is clear, set out in the first paragraph, and explicit as the paper unfolds. The paper should be *written* and should read as easily as possible; as part of that, words have precise meanings and should be used with precision. Make sure you *answer the question* that you have asked: a brilliant answer to a question which is subtly different to the one you started out with is no answer. Finally, keep it *simple*, stupid (KISS): use short, simple words and short sentences. The better a person understands a topic, the more simply he or she can express it, as any lecture by a Nobel Laureate proves (and your readers may not always understand or enjoy complicated words and long sentences anyway). Here are additional points that can help you put those ideas into practice.

Organization. Say very clearly in the beginning which question you are asking yourself, and how you will answer it. Then say how you will go about answering it. Then answer the question in that way. And then conclude by telling the reader what you just have done. Put bluntly, in a paper the reader should know what is going on by the end of the second page, and have an idea of how you will develop your central claim. Such a set-up provides the reader with all the information that he or she needs to evaluate the claims you will substantiate in the body of the paper. If they bother to pick up the paper, readers are, after all, always interested in what you are saying and rarely fundamentally disagree with you; however, you lose points for not saying whatever it is you are trying to say in a clear and transparent manner. This set-up also assures that the reader does not get frustrated by having to read until the end to figure out what the point of the paper was, and then has to reinterpret the material read up until then in light of that question and answer. Do not keep the reader in suspense: magicians may like to pull white rabbits out of a hat at the end of the show, but keeping the punchline until the end is a poor way to organize a paper.

Two considerations follow from this emphasis on organization and structure of the paper and thesis. One is that your introduction to the paper has to be written in two stages. You write it first on the basis of what you know you will write in the body of the paper, but finish it last. In the first stage it exists to get you in the right frame of mind, to force you to think about what you are writing both analytically and synthetically. The introduction should contain the analytical version of your argument, as well as the logical structure of the paper as you are about to write it. In the second stage, when you rewrite the introduction, you look back at what you have written, evaluate what you have not done that you said you would do in the first version, and adjust introduction and body of the text accordingly. It also implies that you should *always* work from an outline. One of the reasons why teachers often ask for such outlines or for tables of contents of theses is that they force you to think about individual elements in the paper or thesis, *as well as* their links with other elements. It also helps you, once you've decided on a workable outline, to use it as a compass, and gauge to what extent you are staying on track. And when everything's written up, you can compare the logic of what you have written with the logic you were trying to work through in the outline. But the outline need not be the first thing you write; in fact, it may be much wiser to jot down ideas randomly first, and then give structure to them by reorganizing them into a coherent outline. That outline will change, of course, as it should; but it helps you keep track of the architecture of your paper and argument while you work on smaller sections.

Real-world questions and the literature. Nothing beats a current policy issue, a big historical problem, or a general widely agreed statement to open a paper. Make sure your research is relevant—and make sure you make clear that it is relevant by setting it up as a big, real-world question. 'Does economic development lead to democratic consolidation or the other way around?', 'Is democracy more likely to consolidate after a violent or after a peaceful transition?' (you could compare countries in Latin America with Central Europe), 'Does international financial integration make redistributive welfare states impossible?' (you could compare two highly integrated economies, both with a retrenched welfare state, or one with a small and one with a large welfare state). The data you will assemble to answer these questions, regardless of whether they come in the form of statistics or cases, then become the observable implications of these questions.

'Gaps in the literature' are manifold and, as I have already said in the first chapter, truly bad reasons for doing research. The literature exists to help you understand an issue, so use it. But do not rely on it for more than that. Very few pieces of advice are as sound as '*forget the literature!*' when you are trying to think through what you want to find out about and what you want to say. Bear in mind that literature reviews are not round-ups of the literature, but exercises in analytical thinking. Put differently, you should critically evaluate the existing literature (and not simply summarize it); however, that implies that you have ideas of your own on what the relevant criteria for evaluation are. Making those explicit will offer you a way to get your own points across. Literature reviews should therefore be very instrumental. Their role is to position your paper in a wider debate on the question you are trying to solve. They are not proof that you have read 'everything' there is to read, and should definitely not reflect your search process in the literature (very few people are interested in that). This implies that you have to cut the literature review down to its essentials, and take it from there. A literature review never has to start from the initial statement of the question, but from where the literature got to when you started (and possibly how and why—although cut that if in doubt). That is something that can be covered in a few pages and, despite common practice, almost never requires a complete chapter in a thesis. Remember that some of the people you criticize will read your paper; be fair towards them, and do not treat them as utter fools. Challenge their ideas, but make sure you can still go for a drink with them afterwards.

Provide roadmaps. The reader should always know where he or she is in the paper and in your plan for the paper. This means regularly summing up what's been done, and a glance at the rest of the paper. One good way of doing this is by providing a short summary and a 'what's to come' sentence at the end of every section that covered an important point (i.e. at least between the introduction and the body of the text that presents empirical material, but sometimes also between subsections). If you discover that there is too much of this road-mapping going on, you can always cut some of it afterwards.

Parsimony and focus. A good paper only answers the question it set out to answer, and it does so with as little material as necessary. All the rest is superfluous baggage, which distracts the reader from your main point. It is hard to let go, but the best advice is nonetheless to evacuate irrelevant information, since it makes the paper harder to read. It is not necessarily lost, since you can always turn it into the basis for another paper. Again, remember that you are making an argument, not trying to show the extent of your knowledge.

One paragraph, one idea. One paragraph should contain one idea. A paragraph should always start by stating the key idea in it, use the balance of the paragraph to develop that key idea, and then wrap it up. More than one idea in one paragraph confuses the reader, especially if the second argument redefines, confines, circumscribes, or (in part) contradicts the first. The best way to resolve this is to break up the paragraph and organize the transition between the two or three of them. Paragraphs can be one sentence or one page long, but try to avoid those which are less than ten and more than twenty-five lines. Short paragraphs that are trying to make a substantive point instead of primarily serving the purpose of transitioning between ideas may leave an impression of thinness, whereas if they become longer, this is often a sign that you are trying to put too many things into one paragraph, and you should consider splitting them.

Referencing. As a rule, a reference should be used to indicate the source of tables and graphs, factual statements that are not common knowledge, and particular support for a contested argument. Your argument can and should build on existing literature, but the logic of what you are trying to say is far more important than any sources you might come up with. Authority arguments are not really arguments, but an attempt to gain intellectual firepower through association with someone else; if you want to make an argument, develop it and then reference it—but never substitute a reference for an argument.

Unfortunately, balancing your sources and your argument has become very complicated recently. While you should definitely avoid over-referencing your papers, the spread of the internet has made most universities very wary of plagiarism and they are taking an increasingly hard line on it (given that plagiarism goes to the heart of our occupation, such a tough attitude should hardly come as a surprise). Knowing how and when to cite a source is part of the learning process that you are engaged in. One particularly useful tip, I think, is to take notes in such a way (e.g. colouring or font) that you can distinguish between what the author says and your reaction to that. And when you lift material from a web site, take good care to cite that site properly. Readers recognize plagiarized texts, and this may well be the only area in life where you are not entirely unreasonably considered guilty until proven innocent.

Citing and listing the literature you used is important, because it tells the reader how you assembled material for the paper. There are standard ways of referencing the literature you used, and you should get acquainted with them. The fastest way is to look at the back cover of journals, where the instructions for authors invariably list house reference styles. References should at least include author, book title or article and journal title, place of publication and publisher (for book), year of publication, and if necessary page numbers (when referencing a particular idea in a book, or when referring to a journal). It is common (and probably easiest) to give author, year, and page numbers in brackets in the text and the full reference in the bibliography afterwards: '(Van Evera 1997); Van Evera, Stephen 1997. *Guide to Methods for Students of Political Science.* Ithaca NY: Cornell University Press'. It is not really that important which style you choose—*de gustibus...*—but that you adopt the style consistently throughout the paper.

Footnoting. Use footnotes sparingly (unless, of course, that is your target journal's referencing style) along the principle that either something is important, and then it should find a place in the text, or it is not, and then it should not be a footnote either. Footnotes should say something which sheds additional light on what you just said, but might break the flow of the text if added in full. Cut every footnote that does not meet these criteria—better still: cut them all, and find a place for relevant pieces of text in the body of the paper itself. Obviously, some disciplines (e.g. law or history) live on footnotes because of the direct information on sources included in them; for these none of these points apply—although you should anyway see if that is also true for analytical rather than case or archive-based papers. Check with editors, supervisors, and friends to figure out what makes most sense in such instances.

Multiple versions. Learn to live with the idea that your first draft is a bad paper which is full of interesting possibilities—the trick is to make the paper a good one and to bring out all the possibilities the paper has. This means that you should rewrite the paper several times, and take comments in seminars, by your supervisors or even in more formal conference settings not just as critiques of your work, but as potentially helpful suggestions to make the paper better. (Many papers would in fact be significantly better if they were read by other students, colleagues, and supervisors and reworked extensively with those critiques in mind. Before you ask, this is not a case of 'do as I say, not as I do': I received extensive comments from seven readers for this short book and have worked hard to incorporate them all, even if that gave me a blinding headache on occasions.) Almost all published academic papers go through at least three fully revised versions, and most have existed in at least five versions. (By the time you read this book, it would have lived in three very different incarnations: one idea for structure that found a premature end, one which was submitted, and one that was revised from the ground up.) You may want to give your paper to a friend for comments: he or she will help you sort out what does and does not work in your paper before you send it around to others. And in case you have made a really bad mistake, it is better for a friend to point that out.

Length. We are a wordy lot, and as a result, papers are often much longer than they should be. My experience is that every paper in its second or third incarnation can easily be cut by about one-third without any substantive implication for the argument. Do it early and definitely before you send it off for review: journals have limited space, and will force you to cut anyway. If you check journals in the standard social sciences (political science, sociology, economics, etc.), you will find that around 7,000 words is often the limit for accepting papers. In some disciplines, long papers are normal: law journals, for example, often will accept papers of a length of 12,000 words or more. Sometimes that may not be a blessing.

Presentation. Use a large font in your draft papers (12 pt will do), at least 1.5 spacing on the computer, and leave relatively wide margins for comments. The world's forests have their rights, but so do the eyes of your readers!

Conclusions. Take some time to think through your conclusion, in the same way that you did for your introduction. A few pointers: re-present the material in light of the way you set up the project in the introduction. Link it back to the broader question and address explicitly how you resolved the puzzle. Spell out clearly what you see as the main theoretical and empirical findings of your research—but do not go over the top by claiming that all of the social sciences should be revised as a result of this paper (go for a drink if the urge to say that gets too strong). Then think of the implications of your research, usually in two areas: policy (i.e. the 'real

Table 5.1 Key ingredients of a bad paper

Bad papers

- Have a messy introduction of a paper
- Present their argument too late
- Un-link the introduction from the rest of the paper
- Ignore the link between introduction and conclusion
- Present an introduction that does not give the structure of the argument
- Are implicit about their research design
- Forget signposts about the structure of the paper at the end of the introduction
- Offer no or unclear signposts
- Let the data speak for themselves
- Let the reader wonder about what the data exactly mean
- Present data that are not directly linked to the core argument
- Decouple the presentation of data from their interpretation
- Write a thin conclusion
- Start a new argument in the conclusion
- Present new data in the conclusion
- Let the conclusion be a summary and nothing else

world'), and research agendas. A combination of an elegant last paragraph and sentence is a nice way to end a paper, but do not agonize too much over its aesthetic qualities. We are researchers, after all, not creative writers.

Bad papers. Despite all these health warnings, bad papers persist. Very often these are papers that never really made it past their first version, and they often land on our desks with the friendly request by a journal editor to write a referee report on this text. Sometimes I get the impression that the editors simply did not do much work of their own, and that the papers are so poor in argument, framing, and presentation that they should have stayed out of my mailbox in the first place: even a cursory glance at that paper would have made it clear that this was not a reviewable paper. Table 5.1 gives you sixteen red alert indicators of a bad paper. Use them to spot when others write them and as a checklist to avoid writing one yourself.

Writing a thesis

Writing a thesis is, as the verb suggests, not a fundamentally different activity from writing a paper. The good news is therefore that the skills you build up by writing papers are practically instantly transferable to thesis writing. A thesis, like a paper, needs an introduction that states the question, the debate, and your argument in light of the data you assembled, and which gives a roadmap to the rest of the text; a body of text that presents the empirical material critically; and a conclusion that ties the empirical material and your argument together. However, a thesis, understood here as a 'big book' thesis, in Dunleavy's words (2003) in his excellent *Authoring a PhD Thesis* (and which I strongly recommend, even to beginning Ph.D. students), is more than just more of the same. A thesis consists of chapters, and chapters are not six to eight stand-alone papers that happen to find themselves between two covers. Chapters have a structure that follows what I presented before on papers: again, a beginning, a middle, and an end. But they also have to relate to each other, become a system in which different parts contribute to a whole which is more than the sum of its parts, and do so in a manageable space: most theses (and practically all books that are derived from theses) have a word limit of about 100,000 words (about one-third longer than this book).

Think of the problem of the thesis in more practical terms as what you have to show for something like four or five years of sustained research on a topic. On the one hand, it has to reflect that time and effort. On the other hand, however, not everything you did during those five years needs to find a way into the thesis. So how do you select from the vast amount of material you have gathered those data that you need? One way is intrinsic relevance, of course—but graduate student myopia is a common, though fortunately easily curable disease. After a few rounds with their supervisors most students know how to drop material that only a few weeks earlier seemed *absolutely* indispensable. But you can make this all a bit easier on everyone by thinking about the structure of your thesis before you start writing: that will help you afterwards in dividing the material into the bits that absolutely need to go in, the bits that might, and those bits that are useless. Your chapter structure should therefore be analytical, not descriptive. If you are comparing two policies in two countries, for example, ask yourself the question if the thesis is better served with two chapters that use the policies as the comparison or with two chapters that use the countries as comparisons. Both are reasonable, but the first will almost certainly force you to be more focused and less wordy. My LSE colleague Patrick Dunleavy (2003) gives the soundest advice I know on how to structure a thesis, and much of what follows is a way of working through his excellent advice (but it is not a substitute, so make the effort to find out for yourself).

The first key principle is *symmetry*: write chapters which are roughly equal in length, with perhaps the introduction and conclusion as exceptions. These chapters are allowed to be shorter or longer than the rest, depending on how you set up the thesis. But the other chapters have to be more or less the same size. What follows now is basic arithmetic: if a thesis is supposed to be about 80–100,000 words long, and you have at least five to six substantive chapters, you are looking at an overall thesis structure of seven to eight chapters of about 10,000 words each, with a margin of error of 1,000–2,000 words. Add another 10–20,000 words for appendices and bibliography, and you're very close if not over the maximum limit. Within the chapters, think of about four sections each consisting of about 2,500 words—roughly the size of essays that you have to write for MA courses. Add it all up: 8 (chapters) × 4 (sections) of 2,500 words each implies that your big thesis consists of about thirty shorter sections the length of the essays that you have been writing up for your MA work. Chopping up the work on a thesis like this has the advantage of making the work associated with writing look considerably less daunting than the tomes you hold in your hands when browsing in the library looking for examples of a thesis. It also forces you to focus hard on each of the subsections as both stand-alone pieces and as parts of a thesis.

The second crucial thing to keep in mind when writing a thesis is *directness*. Ideally, you should come to the point as soon as you can without looking like a bull in a china shop. That means that two preliminary tasks, which are crucial but do not necessarily require much space, should be dealt with as swiftly as possible. A literature review is necessary to tell the reader where you disagree with what others have said about your question. But do not spend a whole chapter reviewing the literature. Practically nothing is as horrible a waste of time for a reader as wading through loads of at best tangentially related points about *what others have said*. Your thesis should reflect your research, and what others have done should be used instrumentally to get you there. Methods chapters are of the same kind. Few theses require a complete chapter on how you got your material, so chuck that idea as soon as it comes up. The basic criterion should be, as Dunleavy (2003) argues, that you give that type of information on a *need to know* basis: what does the reader absolutely need to know to understand where you stand on an issue and what is the contribution that you are making? All else is potentially distracting material. You should therefore force yourself to clear the table (the metaphor will live on) in one, maximum two chapters. Imagine that you sat down for a nice dinner, and half the evening the host is busy clearing the table, after they have put down knives, forks, and plates because it does not seem right. Frustrating, no? Well, the same happens to your readers if you spend two or more chapters not coming to the point in your thesis.

The third and final guideline is *not necessarily to write the thesis in chronological order.* Many students sit down and write chapter 1, chapter 2, and so on until the seven or eight chapters are written. But that is not necessarily the best way to write a thesis. You know where you are headed, and if you took my advice to start writing early, first sections, then papers, and finally the book, you will know more or less what others have said, and how you obtained the material you have. If this is the case, then the best way to start writing is by systematizing that material, and then fan out the thesis from there. This will allow you to calibrate carefully what you say that is new with the introductory material that sets the thesis. Often, in fact, you already have a draft of the section which includes question, literature review, and methodology in the shape of the thesis prospectus that (I hope) you had to write for your department or committee, and which was the ticket for you to embark on doctoral research. Read it again to get your mind focused, then start writing the empirical chapters, and then rewrite the material in the prospectus to fit your substantive chapters. Then have a fresh look at the chapters, and if necessary go back to the introductory chapter that sets up the question. Have you made sure that these two parts of the thesis are seamlessly linked? Repeat this exercise of adjustment of empirical material and set-up until the answer to that question is 'yes'. Then go to the pub for a few drinks.

The single-most relevant piece of advice, though, is to think carefully who you are writing for. Many, possibly most, research students write just for their supervisor. That is a big mistake: yes, you need to convince him or her of the importance of what you are doing, but they are not the ultimate yardstick—and it's too bad for them if they don't know that. You should really have a broader, mostly sympathetic, audience in mind when you write, and should probably also diversify your imaginary audience a bit. Before anything else, think of readers as people who are disposed to be interested in what you do, but are also critical and professional sceptics. One group that should be in there, after your supervisors and other professors in the department, are your fellow graduate students, *especially* those who are not in the thick of your subject. Write in such a way that a smart beginning MA student would understand it. Then think of people who are not used to academic jargon—your parents, say, or your partner, perhaps. They will raise an eyebrow and cough politely when you write words that are unnecessarily difficult and complicated. And then, somewhat counterintuitively, write with the people in mind that you disagree with: if you think you have made a point that X or Y would agree with as a serious point, who else would have a problem with that? In fact, if you can, ask them when you meet them: many—though not necessarily all—of my colleagues are happy to take criticism and point out the problems you may have, without being deeply upset. If they have even a modest understanding of the Lakatosian universe where this book belongs, they know that what you are doing is exactly what should happen: someone builds on what they have done by showing the problem with it. And for you the gains are tremendous: you make contact with someone who was intelligent enough to come up with a set of powerful insights, and who can give you the best counterarguments to yours. If you can beat those by incorporating them into your research design, you have got a pretty much watertight argument.

Conclusions

In a way, writing is possibly the essence of academic research: if we want to influence the way people think about the world—or more modestly become a footnote—we have to have something written, so that others can refer to it. Your ideas, in your mind, are in that sense not really ideas yet. But writing—reproducing—research is something very different from producing research, and there are multiple traps along the way. This chapter looked at how to write papers and a thesis primarily from a conceptual point of view. The question that implicitly organized the first section was how the rules of research design manifest themselves when writing. The second section gave some generic practical advice, building in part on this, on how to write a paper. The third section extended this advice to drafting a thesis. What should have come out, I hope, is that writing is almost an intrinsic part of research, and you learn it in much the same way that you learn what good research is: by doing it a lot, listening carefully to advice, and stealing ideas for structure and organization with your eyes. Writing up your research in a transparent manner, at just the right level of abstraction and with just enough background material that is necessary for the reader to understand what is going on, is a craft which you can learn by doing.

But writing is also a part of research design in another way. The project you embark on is not a linear process, with a clear start and finish. It will often start with a vague sense of facts because of what you have read before, some more or less elaborate conceptual points and possibly ideas about causalities built on those, is then followed by you checking facts and ideas in a more systematic way and restating the initial ideas or searching for new facts, and so on. During that process of redefining your project you are writing the whole time. Your research design takes, as it were, shape through the writing you do. The conclusion is therefore simple: rewrite your project synopsis, doctoral prospectus, research proposal (or whatever it is called or you want to call it) often. Take stock of where you have got to, what it says about what you have done, how what you have done so far fits in the bigger structure of the thesis, check back at what the simplest version of the argument would look like, and see if it all still fits as nicely as it should. As you progress in your project by confronting new facts with old ideas and the other way around, your ideas will become clearer and you will be able to write them up more clearly. And each time you write them up, you become a better writer and a better researcher. While formally the apotheosis of your research, in other words, in the sense that research does not exist without being written up, writing is in fact an intrinsic part of the process of building a research design in the same way that data, cases, method, and ideas are.

FURTHER READING TO CHAPTER 5

Bates (1998), Dunleavy (2003), and Becker (1986) are must-reads once you start to think about writing. George Orwell's 'Politics and the English language' is a remarkable, short piece that should make you think about style, even—especially, perhaps—in academic writing. Additional guidance on writing a paper, in part also captured in the points in this chapter, can be found in Van Evera (1997). Style tips can be handled in two ways: buy or download *The Economist* style guide (whatever you may think about their arguments, they are presented in the best written English on the planet), and read as much as possible good research, if possible also outside your own field (tip: Stephen Jay Gould was a magnificent writer and I learnt a lot from him, not just on paleobiology, but also on philosophy, research design, and baseball).

6 For the Road

Here we are, then. Like you, I am sure, I am happy to have reached the final chapter. You should now have a reasonably good idea of the philosophical foundations of the social sciences, developed a sophisticated understanding of research design, you can critically think about data and cases, and if all goes well, you even have a decent understanding of how to write it all up and tell others about it. I think of this last chapter in the same way as a father who sees his son or daughter off to college: sorry to see them go, but aware that they have to walk on their own now. I am not sure if this is still a tradition the world over, but those were usually the moments when Dad or Mum had a last conversation with the kid who still (just about) lived at home—which then often turned into the first conversation between two adults. This chapter aims to do the same. Rather than summarizing what came before, I want to tie it all together in one collection of points that, I hope, will help you close this book and get down to writing your own.

Starting, finishing, and writing a thesis may, from the vantage point of these pages, have looked like a rational exercise to you. And that invites, especially to those among us with a mild form of Asperger's syndrome, organization. Good—but don't over-organize. Companies are moving away from unnecessary bureaucracy, armies are turning themselves from large body masses into flexible rapid reaction forces, and many governments are decentralizing their decision-making structures. You should not march forcefully in the opposite direction. Remember that research is ultimately a creative process. It may not quite be like jazz, where a piano riff invites the sax to run with it and develop it into something new, but it is not the mindless repetition of a fixed set of tasks either. Your thesis may sometimes seem as nothing more than crossing one unnecessary hurdle after another, and that creativity was left at the entrance gate of the university when you were stupid enough to sign up for this. These hurdles are there for a reason: they make sure that you can walk on your own, can distinguish intelligence from quackery and sophistry, and can convey to your own students how to proceed with a thesis. And even though it may occasionally feel like ticking boxes, research is a creative process at heart: it invites you to think about a problem in a way that no one has ever done before you, use a limited set of tools in ways that have not been combined, and come up with an answer that no one has.

We do not know all that much about creativity. But it is certain to have two key components: passion and surprises. Passion is necessary for several reasons. It gives you drive and energy. The reader recognizes and enjoys it. And many social scientists do what they do because they want to understand and sometimes change the world that they care deeply about. But most of all, passion makes sure that you finish your research. Think of it: from start to finish, that is, from your first year in graduate school to the book that will ultimately result from your thesis, six, seven, sometimes eight or more years pass. That is longer than many marriages these days, so draw your own conclusions.

Surprises are an equally important ingredient of a thesis. From the first time you thought about your topic to the last word you put on paper, things may happen that you had not anticipated: you run into someone at a conference with whom you discuss what you are doing and come home full of new ideas, you read about something tangentially related to what you are doing and find an entirely new way of making sense of your topic, or you discover an under-explored or even ignored set of data which shed an entirely new light on your thesis. All of this has happened to me and to most of my friends and colleagues—the law of averages suggests that they are likely to happen to you as well. What you should avoid are the bad surprises that can set you back for months or even years, and especially those that can ruin your thesis defence. So, some practical pieces of advice.

Talk to as many people as you can about your research. Get two or more supervisors, and use other academics as sounding boards. No one has a monopoly on the truth or on how to do research, not even your supervisor. In fact, many may well disagree with what I wrote in this book. Fine; you can only learn by weighing up different arguments and concluding where you stand on a topic and on which grounds you do so. Remember that your entire intellectual project thrives on intellectual promiscuity.

Think of your thesis as a question, not a topic; questions end with question marks, and statements with full stops. Make sure your project is researchable: do you have access to data, do the variables vary or are they constants, are you clearly delimiting what you are doing in time and space? Can you be wrong—and how would you know if you were? Ask a question that leads to an argument, not to a list of factors that might matter. Is your question sufficiently focused and narrow so that you can reasonably be expected to do it in the four or five years that you have been allotted? Keep in mind, along the way, that you have to be able to explain to your grandmother what you are doing.

Do you have a focused literature review? Since no literature review can ever be complete, stop reading as soon as you can (usually much sooner than you feel you should or could), and start thinking about and discussing what you are trying to do with colleagues, teachers, and others who are interested in what you are doing. Rely on the mini–max principle to define the major positions in the debate: how can you maximize your breadth of the field in as few different positions as possible? Never forget that you decided the question, and that you therefore also decide how to structure the debate. Literature reviews should be analytical, pointed, instrumental, and short: no research question requires two chapters of literature review (usually not even one whole chapter), even if that is the ecological niche where you feel most comfortable. Never use all you have ever read in your thesis. Avoid grand theory; instead go for arguments that are close to the empirical material without being merely descriptive.

Knowing when and how to stop empirical research is as important as starting it. Data-driven research often lends itself better to closure than theory-driven research. Comparative research has a similar advantage over case studies: once you have finished the comparison, you have finished your research. Write early and write a lot. It is the only way you can learn how to do it, and you are going to spend a lot of time doing it anyway, so you might as well frontload the training. Discard empirical material that is not immediately relevant to your thesis. Put it on index cards: strange as it may seem at the start of the project, this will help you avoid a post-natal depression when you submit your thesis. Allow time to have the thesis read by your supervisor(s) and colleagues to check for inconsistencies and lack of clarity. And most of all, 'don't get it right, get it written'. Good luck.

FURTHER READING TO CHAPTER 6

All athletes know that breaks are just as important as practice. So, buy the *Penguin Encyclopedia of Popular Music* and enjoy the music. Locate the nearest café, pub, or bar and know how to get there in five minutes. Run, cycle, play tennis, football . . . anything, really, at least twice a week to take your mind off the Ph.D. Do not forget to read novels. And cherish your friends and partner: a doctoral student's life is very lonely without them.

Social scientists have, on the whole, escaped the caricature of the mad professor with the fiery eyes and the dark-rimmed round glasses intent on destroying the world that the hard sciences have had to cope with—although that may well change after the neo-conservatives have got their hands on US foreign policy (perhaps Kubrick knew the future when making *Dr. Strangelove*?). We rarely need laboratories, so we cannot really be pictured in them in a white coat, and we produce ideas, not all-obliterating nuclear bombs. And even if some of these ideas are deeply racist, sexist, or otherwise offensive, they are almost immediately countered by other ideas. There is one golden rule in science in general: today's crazy ideas can be tomorrow's conventional wisdom, as in the cases of Galilei, Crick and Watson, or Keynes, so we cherish them even if we disagree.

So, taking these points into account: most of social science appears to be a rather benign activity, carried out by people who are full of good intentions. Yet social scientists definitely are no longer lonely savants in small drafty, cold rooms working by candlelight. Instead today it has become, for better or for worse, a highly professionalized endeavour, with training programmes and rites of initiation such as doctoral examinations (one of the considerations, in fact, why many universities have started to teach research design). What follows presents some advice that I have given students over the years about three crucial ways that the professional world in the social sciences today asks you to participate: how to present a paper, how to discuss (and review) a paper (or a book), and how to write up a research proposal.

A. Presenting a paper

Concentrate on getting a few simple points across	You only have a limited time, and you should realize that it is impossible to get everything across. It makes sense, therefore, to reduce your presentation to a limited number of points, which are all directly relevant to the question and topic of your presentation and your overall argument and which are summed up as bullet points in the conclusion. By all means, do not summarize the paper: for those who have read it, this is boring and for the others there may simply be too much detail and too many sidetracks to follow the key argument.

(cont.)

Avoid too much detail	Do not overload the presentation with details. Many details can be summarized in one or two snappy sentences, and that should do. Additional detail can always be given during the discussion afterwards and/or find its way into handouts.
Encourage discussion	It is important to remember the function of your presentation: it should encourage discussion, by making an argument, which then becomes a vehicle for developing a collective understanding of the questions and the topics among the seminar participants, be they other students or colleagues. It is not meant to give a summary statement on the topic. One way to do that is to make a clear argument in the presentation, another is to actively engage what others might think about the question you answer, or to argue why particular positions do not make sense. Discussion is always helped by clear and transparent arguments and statements.
Consider using overheads or PowerPoint to present data	Overheads or PowerPoint are useful ways of helping you with your talk. They can serve two functions. If you speak from notes (but do not read out aloud), you may use the overheads as nudges for yourself. They will allow you to walk around while talking. The other purpose is to use them to present data. Graphs or tables help us see what you mean without you going into detail yourself. If using a table, mark clearly the figure(s) you want the listeners to concentrate on. Text should be large enough for everyone to read them (at least 24 pt). By implication, limit the text to bullet points with a few words. PowerPoint is nice, but too much animation can be distracting, so avoid animation overload.
	Always heed Tufte's advice (2005): very few complex ideas can be expressed in six lines with eight words each (the standard PPT format): consider not using PowerPoint if the gains are too small.
Reading versus speaking from notes	How you talk and present a paper is very different from how you write. The best way to give a talk is to speak from notes. It is more natural, and you can adapt your talk to your audience. However, it requires that you are confident about speaking in public and that you know your subject matter sufficiently well to be able to do so.
	Reading a text is OK as an alternative solution, but then try and write (and read out) spoken English, that is, with interjections that talk to the audience, the use of 'you' in active sentences, etc. Never forget to speak slowly, limit your text to a few points and concentrate at least as much on form as on contents.
Keeping the attention of the audience	A few simple tricks to keep the attention of the audience without doing anything silly:

- look many of them in the eyes (rather than looking only at one person, or looking up at the ceiling or some indeterminate point behind them);
- walking around (especially if the group is sitting in a U-formed table or a circle) and acting as if you are talking to some members of the audience individually helps to make them feel involved and increases their ability and willingness to come along with you;

- a small sarcastic remark or a joke may help to break the tenseness of long sessions. But don't make jokes if you don't feel comfortable: contrived jokes are even worse than a dry talk.

Handouts	Handouts are generally a good idea. They are especially effective if they provide data and graphs, since they add to what you have to say, and if the data are good, then someone can reconstruct large parts of your argument simply by looking at them. For more 'qualitative' talks, handouts with the main points are useful, since they allow for a reconstruction as well. However, make sure that the handout does not deflect attention from your talk (it might be better to give a handout after the talk).
Think about the structure of the presentation	The best way is to start by posing the question that organizes your talk clearly up front, then say how you will answer it and why (in one sentence), and then answer it, fleshing out what is necessary along the way. Your answer and the material you give to support it should be limited to that, made clearly and persuasively, and with only the detail that is necessary to make your point (the rest can follow in the discussion).

B. Discussing or reviewing a paper

Being a discussant of a paper is an important task and you should therefore take it seriously: you will set the stage for the discussion that follows and your comments will usually be the most thought-through reactions that the author receives on that paper. Your comments should concentrate on making a paper better: having a paper discussed at a workshop is an important formal moment in the process of writing a paper, and you are the institutional vehicle for that. When discussing a paper, always be collegial. There are two simple rules to follow: do not do unto others what you would not want to have done unto you; conversely, give the type of comments that you would like to receive yourself (note that the key points below also apply when you are reviewing a paper for a journal or a book for publication).

Think positive	Always start your intervention by pointing out what the paper has tried to do and how it helped you see clearer, moved a debate forward, provided new and interesting empirical material, came to a surprising insight, etc. Almost all papers are potentially good, and it is your duty to make sure that those good points come out clearly. This implies that you always start by reviewing a piece of research on its own terms, and see how well the paper accomplishes what it sets out to do. A critique of the position developed in the paper can wait until after you have done that.

(cont.)

Differentiate your critique	By and large, a paper can be evaluated using three criteria: the central argument, the method, and the organization of the paper. If you differentiate your critique along those lines, you will be very helpful to the author in later stages.
Central argument	Try to capture the central argument of the paper in a few words. Often the author benefits tremendously simply by having you re-state what he or she was trying to say. You may, in fact, use this to tell the author that there is a bigger or slightly different argument hiding in what was written.
	Only after that does it make sense to point out which objections you may have to the argument. This may take the form of pointing out other positions in the debate that the author did not acknowledge, a head-on critique of the central claim of the paper, with which you disagree, or the presentation of disturbing new facts that you have and which fit rather uneasily with the point of the paper. The point of this is not to show that you are smarter than the author, but to tell him or her which weaknesses absolutely should be addressed to move on with the paper.
Method	Explicitly address issues of design and method. Again, the first step in this process is to (re)state what the author is trying to do, and assess it on those terms. Once you've done that, you can start to criticize methodological weaknesses. Try to avoid thinking about a paper with a textbook version of a method in mind: very few research designs actually follow the books. Instead, use the ideals in the methods classes and textbooks as broad reference points, and think through how the paper could be revised to bring the paper closer to the methodological canons. Consider if the data are of the right kind for the question that the paper asked. Always be helpful, that is, think through, in a virtual or real discussion with the author, how methodological problems could be resolved. If you disagree with the method—on principle or for this particular research question—make clear why you disagree. Method is important, but avoid getting bogged down by it.
Organization of the paper	Often the weakest part of conference papers is their organization: papers were written with one particular outline in mind, and as the paper evolved, some of that got lost (perhaps because the material did not lend itself to that anymore). As a discussant, you can be very helpful to the author if you show him or her how to reorganize the paper so that it more accurately reflects the logic of the argument. On organizational issues, you can be very tough: after all, this is the main instrument for the author to make the point, and it is usually the dimension of a paper which is most easily revised. A poorly organized paper is a difficult paper to read, and if the argument is worthwhile, then that is a pity.
Do not dwell on small points	Page-by-page comments are good for email communication, but look pedantic in a public discussion. Only if the paper is full of contradictions does it make sense to (carefully) point that out to the author. Discussing small points only makes sense, really, if they are vital for the paper as a whole—but then they can hardly be called 'small' points.

Further research	Your comments should alert the author to the wider implications of the argument, and by raising those, you perform a valuable duty to the rest of the audience and social science as a whole. Discussing those implications is best done along the lines of 'what the next paper should do' in your presentation. If you can link that to other research you know, you are again very helpful, for the author and others in the workshop or seminar, by drawing together these different strands.
Be succinct	Do all this in five, but certainly less than ten minutes or two to three pages—this implies that during workshops you concentrate on the two or three major points in the critique. Select from among the criticisms you have between the absolutely crucial points and the rest. The discussion afterwards will give you time to develop any other points.
Write out the comments for the author's purpose	Give the author a written version of your comments or at the very least (promise and then actually do) send the author an email with those. You will be more economical when you are forced to write them up, and, since nothing disciplines and organizes thinking as much as writing, you may discover where you were, perhaps, exaggerating your criticisms. Giving the author written comments is also a sign that you took the paper seriously and it will therefore always be appreciated. And since you are both interested in this question or topic, you may well end up having more discussions with the author, at the conference and later on.

C. Research proposals

Many departments today force you to write regular dry-run research proposals that hone your research, and then often make steps in the Ph.D. process dependent on a decent proposal as well. Proposals sound like a chore, one of those things that you need to do to tick boxes. But that is not a particularly useful way of looking at them. They serve one important function: they are a very good way for you to pull together all the threads in your research, and force you to be explicit about your research design. They almost always involve a question, often a puzzle in fact, go on to answers that have been given, allow you to say what is wrong with those and why you think you have a better answer, and then force you to say how you will link your answer to empirical material. In short, they are an embryonic version of your thesis, with questions, research design, and hypotheses where one day answers will be. The main role of a proposal is precisely that: to propel you on towards a thesis by making you state explicitly what you want to do and how.

Whatever else you do with regard to research proposals, read very carefully what Przeworski and Salomon have to say about that.[1] OK, they're talking about getting money for your research, but the way they set it up is that you will only receive decent funding if your proposal is persuasive enough. And the general ideas are true for every proposal you can think of. What I give below is a short, regimented checklist that should get you going. Start with that skeleton outline, and then amend it as the proposal gets read by your colleagues and professors and your ideas take shape. Start early, and take all—yes, all—advice seriously: everyone who reads your proposal wants you to succeed, but they may have doubts about how you're going about it.

Structure of research proposal

Relevance	Why is your research important? Which big issue 'out there' are you trying to understand through your research?
Theory/Model	What are you trying to explain? What is your empirical question or puzzle? What are the causal claims you are interested in? What is the simplest model you can propose? Why do you prefer this model/argument to others?
Method	How are you trying to explain? What is your basic research design? How close is it to some of the standard ones discussed here (critical case, comparative design, etc.)?
Universe	On what bases are units of observation—countries, regions, policies, etc.—selected? Are they similar or dissimilar in terms of what you are trying to find out? Time period: which historical period(s) will you analyse and why? Will you do so by looking at the effects of similar shocks or events? Or by examining different historical periods within/across countries? Assure your case has both a beginning and an end.
Data and data sources	Where will you get the necessary information?

---

[1] The text by Przeworski and Salomon can be found at http://fellowships.ssrc.org/art_of_writing_proposals/.

BIBLIOGRAPHY

Abraham, David. 1981. *The Collapse of the Weimar Republic: Political Economy and Crisis.* Princeton, NJ: Princeton University Press.

Adcock, Robert and David Collier. 2001. 'Measurement Validity: A Shared Standard for Qualitative and Quantitative Research', *American Political Science Review,* 95 (September): 529–46.

Allison, Graham T. 1971. *Essence of Decision: Explaining the Cuban Missile Crisis.* Boston, MA: Little Brown.

Bagnasco, Arnaldo. 1977. *Tre Italia: la problematica territoriale dello sviluppo italiano.* Bologna: Il Mulino.

Baker, Dean, Andrew Glyn, David R. Howell, and John Schmitt. 2004. 'Labor Market Institutions and Unemployment: A Critical Assessment of the Cross-Country Evidence', in D. Howell, *Fighting Unemployment: The Limits of Free Market Orthodoxy.* Oxford: Oxford University Press.

Bassanini, Andrea and Romain Duval. 2006. 'Employment Patterns in OECD Countries: Reassessing the Role of Policies and Institutions'. OECD Working Paper 486.

Bates, Robert. 1998. 'Introduction', in Robert Bates, Avner Greif, et al. *Analytical Narratives.* Princeton, NJ: Princeton University Press.

Batstone, Eric, Ian Boraston, and Stephen Frenkel. 1978. *The Social Organization of Strikes.* Oxford: Blackwell.

Becker, Howard. 1986. *Writing for Social Scientists: How to Start and Finish Your Thesis, Book, or Article.* Chicago: University of Chicago Press.

Birn, Ruth B. and Volker Riess. 1997. 'Revising the Holocaust: Review of Goldhagen's *Hitler's Willing Executioners*', *The Historical Journal,* 40(1): 195–215.

Block, Fred L. 1990. *Postindustrial Possibilities: A Critique of Economic Discourse.* Berkeley, CA: University of California Press.

Brady, Henry E. and David Collier (eds.). 2004. *Rethinking Social Inquiry: Diverse Tools, Shared Standards.* Lanham, MD: Rowman & Littlefield.

Braumoeller, Bear F. and Gary Goertz. 2000. 'The Methodology of Necessary Conditions', *American Journal of Political Science,* 44(4): 844–58.

Bronk, Richard. 2009. *The Romantic Economist: Imagination in Economics.* Cambridge: Cambridge University Press.

Clark, William Roberts, Michael J. Gilligan, and Matt Golder. 2006. 'A Simple Multivariate Test for Asymmetric Hypotheses', *Political Analysis,* 14: 311–31.

Crouch, Colin. 2005. *Capitalist Diversity and Change: Recombinant Governance and Institutional Entrepreneurs.* Oxford, New York: Oxford University Press.

Cusack, Thomas R. and Lutz Engelhardt. 2002. 'The PGL File Collection: File Structures and Procedures', available at http://www.wzb.eu/mp/mps/people/cusack/pdf/PGL_Structures_and_Procederes_ce.pdf (accessed on 6 January 2009).

Dunleavy, Patrick. 2003. *Authoring a PhD: How to Plan, Draft, Write and Finish a Doctoral Thesis or Dissertation.* Basingstoke: Palgrave MacMillan.

Durkheim, Emile. 1990 (1897). *Suicide: A Study in Sociology.* London: Free Press.

Eckstein, Harry. 1975. 'Case Study and Theory in Political Science', in Fred Greenstein and Nelso Polsby (eds.), *Handbook of Political Science.* Reading, MA: Addison-Wesley.

Elster, Jon. 1989. *Nuts and Bolts for the Social Sciences.* Cambridge: Cambridge University Press.

Emigh, Rebbeca J. 1997. 'The Power of Negative Thinking: The Use of Negative Case Methodology in the Development of Sociological Theory', *Theory and Society,* 26: 649–84.

Esping-Andersen, Gosta. 1990. *The Three Worlds of Welfare Capitalism.* Cambridge: Polity Press.

Foucault, Michel. 1970. *The Order of Things: An Archaeology of the Human Sciences.* London: Tavistock Publications.

Gerring, John. 2001. 'What is a Case Study and What is it Good For?', *American Political Science Review,* 98(2): 341–54.

—— 2007. *Case Study Research: Principles and Practices.* New York: Cambridge University Press.

Goertz, Gary. 2003. *Assessing the Importance of Necessary or Sufficient Conditions in Fuzzy-set Social Science,* manuscript, Department of Political Science, University of Arizona.

Goldhagen, Daniel Jonah. 1996. *Hitler's Willing Executioners: Ordinary Germans and the Holocaust.* London: Little, Brown.

Gould, Steven Jay. 1990. *Wonderful Life: The Burgess Shale and the Nature of History.* New York: Norton.

Hall, Peter A. 1990. 'Helpful Hints for Writing Dissertations in Comparative Politics', *PS: Political Science and Politics,* 23(4): 596–98.

—— 2004. 'Aligning Ontology and Methodology in Comparative Research', in James Mahoney and Dietrich Rueschemeyer, *Comparative Historical Analysis in the Social Sciences.* Cambridge: Cambridge University Press.

—— and David Soskice (eds.). 2001. *Varieties of Capitalism: The Institutional Foundations of Competitiveness.* Oxford: Oxford University Press.

Hamilton, Richard F. 1996. *The Social Misconstruction of Reality: Validity and Verification in the Scholarly Community.* New Haven, CT: Yale University Press.

Huff, Darrell. 1991. *How to Lie with Statistics.* Harmondsworth: Penguin.

King, Gary, Robert Keohane, and Sidney Verba. 1994. *Designing Social Inquiry.* Princeton, NJ: Princeton University Press.

King, Lawrence. 2007. 'Central European Capitalism in Comparative Perspective', in Bob Hancké, Martin Rhodes, and Mark Thatcher (eds.), *Beyond Varieties of Capitalism: Conflict, Contradiction and Complementarities in the European Economy.* Oxford: Oxford University Press.

Kittel, Bernard. 2006. 'A Crazy Methodology? On the Limits of Macroquantitative Social Science Research', *International Sociology*, 21(5): 647–78.

Korpi, Walter. 1983. *The Democratic Class Struggle.* London: Routledge & Kegan Paul.

Kuhn, Thomas S. 1962. *The Structure of Scientific Revolutions.* Chicago, IL: University of Chicago Press.

Lakatos, Imre. 1970. 'Falsification and the Methodology of Scientific Research Programmes', in Imre Lakatos and Alan Musgrave (eds.), *Criticism and the Growth of Knowledge.* Cambridge: Cambridge University Press, 116–22, 132–8.

Latour, Bruno. 1987. *Science in Action: How to Follow Scientists and Engineers through Society.* Milton Keynes: Open University Press.

Layard, P. Richard G. 2005. *Happiness: Lessons from a New Science.* London: Allen Lane.

—— Stephen Nickell, and Richard Jackman. 1991. *Unemployment: Macroeconomic Performance and the Labour Market.* Oxford: Oxford University Press.

Levitt, Steven D. 2005. *Freakonomics: A Rogue Economist Explores the Hidden Side of Everything.* New York: William Morrow.

Lieberman, Evan S. 2005. 'Nested Analysis as a Mixed-Method Strategy for Comparative Research', *American Political Science Review*, 99(3): 435–52.

Lipset, Seymour Martin, Martin A. Trow, and James S. Coleman. 1956. *Union Democracy: The Internal Politics of the International Typographical Union.* Glencoe, IL.: Free Press.

Locke, Richard M. and Kathleen Thelen. 1995. 'Apples and Oranges Revisited: Contextualized Comparison and the Study of Comparative Labor Politics.' *Politics and Society*, 23(3): 337–68.

Michels, Robert. 1915. *Political Parties: A Sociological Study of the Oligarchical Tendencies of Modern Democracy.* New York: Dover.

McKeown, Timothy. 2004. 'Case Studies and the Limits of the Statistical Worldview', in David Collier and Henry Brady (eds.), *Rethinking Social Inquiry: Diverse Tools, Shared Standards.* Lanham, MD: Rowman & Littlefield.

Mills, C. Wright. 1956. *The Power Elite.* London: Oxford University Press.

Moore, Barrington. 1967. *Social Origins of Dictatorship and Democracy: Lord and Peasant in the Making of the Modern World.* London: Allen Lane.

Nickell, Steve and Jan Van Ours. 2000. 'Falling Unemployment: The Dutch and British Cases'. *Economic Policy*, Vol. 30: 137–175.

Pierson, Paul. 2004. *Politics in Time: History, Institutions, and Social Analysis.* Princeton, NJ: Princeton University Press.

Popper, Karl. 1959. *The Logic of Scientific Discovery.* London: Hutchinson.

—— 1989. *Conjectures and Refutations: The Growth of Knowledge.* London: Routledge.

Przeworski, Adam and Henry Teune. 1970. *The Logic of Comparative Social Inquiry.* New York: Wiley.

—— and Frank Salomon. *The Art of Writing Proposals: Some Candid Suggestions for Applicants to Social Science Research Council Competitions.* New York: SSRC. Available at http://fellowships.ssrc.org/art_of_writing_proposals/ (accessed on 6 January 2009).

Ragin, Charles C. 1987. *The Comparative Method: Moving beyond Qualitative and Quantitative Strategies.* Berkeley, CA: University of California Press.

Ragin, Charles. 2000. *Fuzzy-set Social Science.* Chicago, IL: University of Chicago Press.

Ragin, Charles. 2008. *Redesigning Social Inquiry: Fuzzy-sets and Beyond.* Chicago, IL: University of Chicago Press.

Rohlfing, Ingo. 2008. 'What You See and What You Get: The Pitfalls of Nested Analysis in Comparative Research', *Comparative Political Studies,* 41(11): 1492–514.

Rueschemeyer Dietrich, Evelyne Huber Stephens, and John D. Stephens. 1991. *Capitalist Development and Democracy.* Cambridge: Polity Press.

Sacks, Oliver. 1986. *The Man Who Mistook his Wife for a Hat.* London: Picador.

Schmitter, Philippe. 2008. 'The Design of Social and Political Research', in Donatella Della Porta and Michael Keating, *Approaches and Methodologies in the Social Sciences: A Pluralist Perspective.* Cambridge: Cambridge University Press.

Schneider, Carsten Q. and Claudius, Wagemann. 2007. 'Qualitative Comparative Analysis (QCA) und Fuzzy Sets. Ein Lehrbuch für Anwender und jene, die es werden wollen', Opladen/Farmington Hills: Verlag Barbara Budrich.

Selznick, Philip. 1949. *TVA and the Grass Roots: A Study in the Sociology of Formal Organization.* Berkeley, CA: University of California Press.

Shalev, Michael. 2007. 'Limits and Alternatives to Multiple Regression in Comparative Research', *Comparative Social Research,* 24: 261–308.

Shively, W. Phillips. 2002. *The Craft of Political Research.* Upper Saddle River, NJ: Prentice Hall.

Skocpol, Theda. 1979. *States and Social Revolutions: A Comparative Analysis of France, Russia and China.* Cambridge: Cambridge University Press.

—— 1984. 'Emerging Agendas and Recurrent Research Strategies in Historical Sociology', in T. Skocpol (ed.), *Vision and Method in Historical Sociology.* Cambridge: Cambridge University Press.

Stiglitz, Joseph. 1999. 'Whither Reform? Ten Years of the Transition'. Keynote Address, World Bank Annual Conference on Development Economics.

Streeck, Wolfgang. 1996. 'Lean Production in the German Automobile Industry? A Test Case for Convergence Theory', in Suzanne Berger and Ronald Dore (eds.), *National Diversity and Global Capitalism*. Ithaca, NY: Cornell University Press, 138–70.

—— and Kathleen Thelen. 2004. *Beyond Continuity: Institutional Change in Advanced Political Economies*. Oxford: Oxford University Press.

Thomas, William I. and Florian Znaniecki. 1927. *The Polish Peasant in Europe and America*. New York: Knopf.

Tufte, Edward R. 2001. *The Visual Display of Quantitative Information*. Cheshire, CT: Graphics Press.

—— 2005. 'PowerPoint Does Rocket Science—and Better Techniques for Technical Reports'. http://www.edwardtufte.com/bboard/q-and-a-fetch-msg?msg_id=0001yB& topic_id=1 (accessed on 6 January 2009).

Turner, Henry A. 1985. *German Big Business and the Rise of Hitler*. Oxford: Oxford University Press.

Turner, Lowell. 1991. *Democracy at Work: Changing World Markets and the Future of Labor Unions*. Ithaca, NY: Cornell University Press.

Van Evera, Stephen. 1997. *Guide to Methods for Students of Political Science*. Ithaca, NY: Cornell University Press.

Webb, Eugene. 1966. *Unobtrusive Measures: Nonreactive Research in the Social Sciences*. Chicago, IL: Rand McNally.

Weber, Max. 1976. *The Protestant Ethic and the Spirit of Capitalism*. London: Allen and Unwin.

Wood, Stewart. 2001. 'Business, Government and Patterns of Labour Market Policy in Britain and the Federal Republic of Germany', in Peter Hall and David Soskice, *Varieties of Capitalism: The Institutional Foundations of Comparative Advantage*. Oxford: Oxford University Press.

◻ INDEX

Lightning Source UK Ltd.
Milton Keynes UK
UKOW04f0513040914

238046UK00001B/3/P